Parades and Protests
An Annotated Bibliography

John Bell

Institute for Conflict Research

First Published October 2007

Institute for Conflict Research
North City Business Centre
2 Duncairn Gardens
Belfast BT15 2GG
Tel: +44 (0)28 9074 2682
Email: info@conflictresearch.org.uk
Web: www.conflictresearch.org.uk

Belfast Interface Project
Third Floor
109-113 Royal Avenue
Belfast BT1 1FF
Tel: +44 (0)28 9024 2828
Email: info@belfastinterfaceproject.org
Web: www.belfastinterfaceproject.org

ISBN: 978-0-9552259-3-2

This project has been funded through the Belfast City Council Good
Relations Programme Unit and the Community Relations Council.

Produced by:
three creative company ltd

Table of Contents

Page

1. Bell, Desmond (1990) Acts of Union: Youth Culture and   15
   Sectarianism in Northern Ireland.
2. British-Irish Inter-Parliamentary Body (2001) The Cultural   18
   Significance of Parades.
3. Bryan, Dominic (1998) Ireland's very own Jurassic Park.   19
4. Bryan, Dominic (1999) The Right to March: Parading a Loyal   20
   Protestant Identity in Northern Ireland.
5. Bryan, Dominic (2000) Orange Parades: The Politics of   21
   Ritual and Control.
6. Bryan, Dominic (2000) Drumcree and 'The Right to March':   25
   Orangeism, Ritual and Politics in Northern Ireland.
7. Bryan, Dominic (2005) Fanatics, Mobs and Terrorists: The   26
   Dynamics of Orange Parades in Northern Ireland.
8. Bryan, Dominic (2006) 'Traditional' Parades, Conflict and   27
   Change: Orange Parades and other Rituals in Northern
   Ireland, 1960-2000.
9. Bryan, Dominic; Fraser, T.G. and Dunn, Seamus (1995)   28
   Political Rituals: Loyalist Parades in Portadown.
10. Bryan, Dominic and Jarman, Neil (1997) Parading Tradition, 31
    Protesting Triumphalism: Utilising Anthropology in Public
    Policy.
11. Bryan, Dominic and Jarman, Neil (1999) Independent   32
    Intervention: Monitoring the police, parades and public
    order.
12. Bryett, Keith (1997) Does Drumcree '96 tell us anything   36
    about the RUC?
13. Buckley, Anthony D., and Kenney, Mary Catherine (1995)   37
    Negotiating Identity: Rhetoric, Metaphor and Social Drama
    in Northern Ireland.
14. Cecil, Roseanne (1993) The Marching Season in Northern   38
    Ireland: An Expression of a Politico-Religious Identity.
15. Committee on the Administration of Justice (1996) The   39
    Misrule of Law: A Report on the policing of events during the
    summer of 1996 in Northern Ireland.
16. Committee on the Administration of Justice (1997) Policing 42
    the Police: A Report on the policing of events during the
    summer of 1997 in Northern Ireland.
17. de Rosa, Ciro (1998) Playing Nationalism.   43

18. Dickson, Bruce and O'Brien, Martin (eds.) (2003) Civil Liberties in Northern Ireland: The CAJ Handbook. Fourth Edition.   44
19. Dunn, Seamus (2000) Bloody Sunday and its Commemorative Parades.   45
20. Dudley-Edwards, Ruth (1999) The Faithful Tribe. An Intimate Portrait of the Loyal Institutions.   46
21. Farrell, Sean (2000) Rituals and Riots: Sectarian Violence and Political Culture in Ulster 1784-1886.   49
22. Fraser, T. G. (2000) The Apprentice Boys and Relief of Derry Parades   52
23. Fraser, Grace and Morgan, Valerie (2000) 'Miracle on the Shankill': The Peace March and Rally of 28th August 1976.   53
24. Garvaghy Residents (1999) Garvaghy: A Community Under Siege.   54
25. Hadden, Tom and Donnelly, Anne (1997) The Legal Control of Marches in Northern Ireland.   55
26. Hall, Michael (1998) (ed.) Springfield Inter-community Development Project: Report of a series of seminars.   58
27. Hall, Michael (2004) (ed.) Exploring the Marching Issue: Views from Nationalist North Belfast.   59
28. Hamilton, Michael (2001) Determining the Right to March.   60
29. Hamilton, Michael (2005) Parade related protests: is it the 'taking part' that counts?   61
30. Hamilton, Michael (2005) Freedom of Assembly, Consequential Harms and the Rule of Law: Liberty-limiting Principles in the Context of Transition.   61
31. Hamilton, Michael; Jarman, Neil and Bryan, Dominic (2001) Parades, Protests and Policing: A Human Rights Framework.   62
32. Hamilton, Michael and Bryan, Dominic (2006) Deepening Democracy? Dispute System Design and the Mediation of Contested Parades in Northern Ireland.   64
33. Human Rights Watch/Helsinki Watch (1997) To Serve Without Favor: Policing, Human Rights and Accountability in Northern Ireland.   66
34. Irish Parades Emergency Committee (1998) Observors Guidebook.   68
35. Irish Parades Emergency Committee and Brehon Law Society (2005) Sectarianism on Parade: Orange Parades in Northern Ireland: Summer 2005 International Observors' Report.   68
36. Jarman, Neil (1993) Intersecting Belfast: Landscape, Politics and Perspectives.   70

37. Jarman, Neil (1997) Material Conflicts: Parades and Visual Displays in Northern Ireland.   71

38. Jarman, Neil (1998) Material of Culture, Fabric of Identity.   75

39. Jarman, Neil (1999) Commemorating 1916, Celebrating Difference: Parading and Painting in Belfast.   76

40. Jarman, Neil (1999) Regulating Rights and Managing Public Order: Parade Disputes and the Peace Process, 1995-1998.   78

41. Jarman, Neil (2000) For God and Ulster: Blood and Thunder Bands and Loyalist Political Culture.   79

42. Jarman, Neil (2003) From Outrage to Apathy? The Disputes over Parades, 1995-2003.   80

43. Jarman, Neil and Bryan, Dominic (1996) Parade and Protest: A Discussion of Parading Disputes in Northern Ireland.   82

44. Jarman, Neil and Bryan, Dominic (1998) From Riots to Rights: Nationalist Parades in the North of Ireland.   85

45. Jarman, Neil; Bryan, Dominic; Caleyron, Nathalie and de Rosa, Ciro (1998) Politics in Public: Freedom of Assembly and the Right to Protest: A Comparative Analysis.   89

46. Jarman, Neil and Bryan, Dominic (2000) Stewarding Crowds and Managing Public Safety: Developing a Co-ordinated Policy for Northern Ireland..   91

47. Jarman, Neil and Bryan, Dominic (2000) Green Parades in an Orange State: Nationalist and Republican Commemorations and Demonstrations from Partition to the Troubles, 1920-1970.   92

48. Jeffrey, Keith (2000) Parades, Police and Government in Northern Ireland, 1922-1969.   93

49. Jones, David; Kane, James; Wallace, Robert; Sloan, Douglas and Courtney, Brian (1996) The Orange Citadel: A History of Orangeism in Portadown District.   93

50. Kelly, Gráinne (1998) (ed.) Mediation in Practice: A Report of the Art of Mediation Project.   94

51. Kennaway, Brian (2006) The Orange Order: A Tradition Betrayed.   96

52. Larsen, Sidsel Saugestad (1982) The two sides of the house: identity and social organisation in Kilbroney, Northern Ireland.   98

53. Larsen, Sidsel Saugestad (1982) The Glorious Twelfth: the politics of legitimation in Kilbroney.   98

54. Loftus, Belinda (1994) Mirrors: Orange and Green.   100

55. Lucy, Gordon (1996) Stand-off! Drumcree: July 1995 and 1996.   102

56. Lucy, Gordon and McClure, Elaine (1997) (eds.) The Twelfth: What it means to me.   103

57. McAuley, Imelda (1998) Reforming the Law on Contentious Parades in Northern Ireland.   104

58. Miller, Deborah J. (2004) Walking the Queens Highway: Ideology and Cultural Landscape in Northern Ireland.   105

59. Montgomery; Graham and Witten, Richard J. (1995) The Order on Parade.   106

60. Northern Ireland Affairs Committee: The Parades Commission and Public Processions (Northern Ireland) Act 1998. Volume I (2004)   107

61. Northern Ireland Forum for Political Dialogue: Standing Committee A (1997) Review of the Parades Issue in Northern Ireland: Volume 1.   109

62. Northern Ireland Forum for Political Dialogue: Standing Committee A (1997) Review of the Parades Issue in Northern Ireland: Volume 2.   110

63. Northern Ireland Office Steering Group, Second Report (2001) Patten Report Recommendations 69 and 70 Relating to Public Order Equipment: A Research Programme into Alternative Policing Approaches Towards the Management of Conflict.   111

64. Northern Ireland Office Steering Group Third Report (2002) Patten Report Recommendations 69 and 70 Relating to Public Order Equipment: A Research Programme into Alternative Policing Approaches Towards The Management Of Conflict.   114

65. Northern Ireland Policing Board (2005) Human Rights: Monitoring the Compliance of the Police Service of Northern Ireland with the Human Rights Act 1998: Annual Report 2005.   115

66. Northern Ireland Policing Board (2005) Monitoring the Compliance of the Police Service of Northern Ireland with the Human Rights Act 1998: Report on the Policing of the Ardoyne Parades 12th July 2005, and the Whiterock Parade 10th September 2005.   118

67. Northern Ireland Policing Board (2006) Monitoring the Compliance of the Police Service of Northern Ireland with the Human Rights Act 1998: Human Rights: Annual Report 2006.   119

68. North Report (1997) Independent Review of Parades and Marches.   120

69. Orr, Sir John (2005) Review of Marches and Parades in Scotland. — 122

70. Parades Commission (2005) Public Processions and Related Protest Meetings: Guidelines, A Code of Conduct and Procedural Rules. — 124

71. Parades Commission (2006) Parades Commission 2006 – 2007: Parading in a Peaceful Northern Ireland: Forward View and Review of Procedures. — 125

72. Pat Finucane Centre (1995) One Day in August. — 126

73. Pat Finucane Centre (1996) In the Line of Fire: Derry, July 1996. — 128

74. Pat Finucane Centre (1997) For God and Ulster: An Alternative Guide to the Loyal Orders. — 129

75. PeaceWatch Ireland (1997) Looking into the Abyss: Witnesses' Report from Garvaghy Road, Portadown. July 4th - July 6th 1997. — 130

76. Police Ombudsman for Northern Ireland (2002) Baton Rounds Report 2002. — 130

77. Police Ombudsman for Northern Ireland (2005) Baton Rounds Report 2005. — 131

78. Purdie, Bob (1990) Politics in the Streets: The Origins of the Civil Rights Movement in Northern Ireland. — 131

79. Quigley, Sir George (2002) Report: Review of the Parades Commission and Public Processions (Northern Ireland) Act 1998. — 135

80. Radford, Katy (2001) Drum rolls and gender roles in Protestant marching bands in Belfast. — 137

81. Radford, Katy (2004) Protestant Women – Protesting Faith: Tangling Secular and Religious Identity in Northern Ireland. — 138

82. Ryder, Chris and Kearney, Vincent (2001) Drumcree: The Orange Order's Last Stand. — 139

83. Salhany, Susan (2007) Exposing Foucault's Two Rituals: Considering the Symbolic Dimension of Government. — 140

84. Tonkin, Elizabeth and Bryan, Dominic (1996) Political Ritual: Temporality and Tradition. — 141

85. United States Institute of Peace (No date) Simulation on Northern Ireland: One Step at a Time – The Derry March and Prospects for Peace. — 142

86. Walker, Brian (1996) Dancing to History's Tune: History, myth and politics in Ireland. — 142

87. Witherow, Jacqueline (2005) The 'War on Terrorism' and Protestant Parading Bands in Northern Ireland. — 142

Publications in Chronological Order

Year	Publication	Page
1982	Larsen, S. *The Glorious Twelfth.*	98
1982	Larsen, S. *The two sides of the house.*	98
1990	Bell, D. *Acts of Union.*	15
1990	Purdie, B. *Politics in the Streets.*	131
1993	Cecil, R. *The Marching Season in Northern Ireland.*	38
1993	Jarman, N. *Intersecting Belfast.*	70
1994	Loftus, B. *Mirrors: Orange and Green.*	100
1995	Bryan, D; Fraser, T.G and Dunn, S. *Political Rituals.*	28
1995	Buckley, A. and Kenney, M. C. *Negotiating Identity.*	37
1995	Montgomery, G. W and Witten, R. *The Order on Parade.*	106
1995	Pat Finucane Centre *One Day in August.*	126
1996	Committee on the Administration of Justice *The Misrule of Law.*	39
1996	Jarman, N. and Bryan, D. *Parade and Protest.* 1996	82
	Jones, D., Kane, S. J., Wallace, R., Sloan, D., and Courtney, B. *The Orange Citadel.*	93
1996	Lucy, G. *Stand-off! Drumcree.*	102
1996	Pat Finucane Centre *In the Line of Fire.*	128
1996	Tonkin, E. and Bryan, D. *Political Ritual.*	141
1996	Walker, B. *Dancing to History's Tune.*	142
1997	Bryan, D. and Jarman, N. *Parading tradition, protesting triumphalism.*	31
1997	Bryett, K. *Does Drumcree '96 tell us anything about the RUC?*	36
1997	Committee on the Administration of Justice *Policing the Police.*	42
1997	Hadden, T. and Donnelly, A. *The Legal Control of Marches in Northern Ireland.*	55
1997	Human Rights Watch/Helsinki *Watch To Serve Without Favor.*	66
1997	Jarman, N. *Material Conflicts.*	71
1997	Lucy, G. and McClure, E. *The Twelfth.*	103
1997	Northern Ireland Forum for Political Dialogue: *A Review of the Parades Issue in Northern Ireland: Volume 1.*	109

1997   Northern Ireland Forum for Political Dialogue: *A*   110
        Review of the Parades Issue in Northern Ireland: Volume 2.

1997   North, P. *Independent Review of Parades and Marches.*   120
1997   Pat Finucane Centre *For God and Ulster.*   129
1997   Peace Watch Ireland. *Looking into the Abyss.* 1998   130
        Bryan, D. *Ireland's very own Jurassic Park.*   19
1998   de Rosa, C. *Playing Nationalism.*   43
1998   Hall, M. *Springfield Inter-community Development Project.*   58

1998   Irish Parades Emergency Committee *Observors*   68
        Guidebook.
1998   Jarman, N. *Material of Culture, Fabric of Identity.*   75
1998   Jarman, N. and Bryan, D. *From Riots to Rights.* 1998   85
        Jarman, N., Bryan, D., Caleyron, N. and de Rosa, C.   89
        Politics in Public
1998   Kelly, G. *Mediation in Practice.*   94
1998   McAuley, I. *Reforming the Law on Contentious Parades in*   104
        Northern Ireland.
1999   Bryan, D. *The Right to March.*   25
1999   Bryan, D. and Jarman, N. *Independent Intervention.*   32
1999   Dudley-Edwards, R. *The Faithful Tribe.*   46
1999   Garvaghy Residents *Garvaghy: A Community Under Siege.*   54

1999   Jarman, N. *Commemorating 1916, Celebrating Difference.*   76

1999   Jarman, N. *Regulating Rights and Managing Public Order.*   78

2000   Bryan, D. *Orange Parades.*   21
2000   Bryan, D. *Drumcree and the Right to March.*   25
2000   Dunn, S. *Bloody Sunday and its Commemorative Parades.*   45

2000   Farrell, S. *Rituals and Riots.*   49
2000   Fraser, T.G. *The Apprentice Boys and the Relief of Derry*   52
        Parades.
2000   Fraser, G. and Morgan, V. *Miracle on the Shankill.*   53
2000   Jarman, N. *For God and Ulster.*   79
2000   Jarman, N. and Bryan, D. *Stewarding Crowds and*   91
        Managing Public Safety: Developing a Co-ordinated Policy
        for Northern Ireland.
2000   Jarman, N. and Bryan D. *Green Parades in an Orange*   92
        State.

2000	Jeffrey, K. *Parades, Police and Government in Northern Ireland.*	93
2001	British-Irish Inter-Parliamentary Body *The Cultural Significance of Parades.*	18
2001	Hamilton, M. *Determining the Right to March.* 2001	60
	Hamilton, M., Jarman, N. and Bryan, D. *Parades, Protests and Policing.*	62
2001	Northern Ireland Office Steering Group Second Report *Patten Report Recommendations 69 and 70 Relating to Public Order Equipment.*	111
2001	Radford, K. *Drum rolls and gender roles.*	137
2001	Ryder, C. and Kearney, V. *Drumcree.*	139
2002	Northern Ireland Office Steering Group Third Report *Patten Report Recommendations 69 and 70 Relating to Public Order Equipment.*	114
2002	Police Ombudsman for Northern Ireland *Baton Rounds Report 2002.*	130
2002	Quigley, G. *Review of the Parades Commission and Public Processions (Northern Ireland) Act 1998.*	135
2003	Dickson, B. and O'Brien, M. *Civil Liberties in Northern Ireland.*	44
2003	Jarman, N. *From Outrage to Apathy?*	80
2004	Hall, M. *Exploring the Marching Issue.*	59
2004	Miller, D. *Walking the Queen's Highway.*	105
2004	Northern Ireland Affairs Committee *The Parades Commission and Public Processions (Northern Ireland) Act 1998.*	107
2004	Radford, K. *Protestant Women – Protesting Faith.*	138
2005	Bryan, D. *Fanatics, Mobs and Terrorists.*	26
2005	Hamilton, M. *Parade related protests.*	61
2005	Hamilton, M. *Freedom of Assembly, Consequential Harms and the Rule of Law.*	61
2005	Irish Parades Emergency Committee and Brehon Law Society *Sectarianism on Parade.*	68
2005	Northern Ireland Policing Board *Monitoring the Compliance of the PSNI with the Human Rights Act 1998.*	115
2005	Northern Ireland Policing Board *Report on the Policing of the Ardoyne Parades 12th July 2005, and the Whiterock Parade 10th September 2005.*	118
2005	Orr, J. *Review of Marches and Parades in Scotland.*	122
2005	Parades Commission *Public Processions and Related Protest Meetings.*	124

2005	Parades Commission *Parading in a Peaceful Northern Ireland.*	125
2005	Police Ombudsman for Northern Ireland *Baton Rounds Report 2005.*	131
2005	Witherow, J. *The 'War on Terrorism' and Protestant Parading Bands in Northern Ireland.*	142
2006	Bryan, D. *'Traditional' Parades, Conflict and Change.*	27
2006	Hamilton, M. and Bryan, D. *Deepening Democracy?*	64
2006	Kennaway, B. *The Orange Order.*	96
2006	Northern Ireland Policing Board *Monitoring the Compliance of the PSNI with the Human Rights Act 1998.*	119
2007	Salhany, S. *Exposing Foucault's Two Rituals.*	140
No Date	United States Institute of Peace *Simulation on Northern Ireland.*	142

Preface

Belfast Interface Project (BIP) is a membership organisation committed to informing and supporting the development of effective regeneration strategies in Belfast's interface areas.

One of the aims of BIP is to enhance and develop the knowledge base regarding Belfast's interface areas. Given that parades and parade-related protests and disputes have generated division in recent years and that this division has translated into conflict in a number of interface areas, it seemed appropriate to commission the Institute for Conflict Research to bring together within one document a collection of abstracts of existing literature on this subject.

This document aims to make this body of literature more accessible to those who may be interested in this area, including our members and key stakeholders. The collection is indexed both by author and chronology and is also available for download from our website at www.belfastinterfaceproject.org.

Accompanying this document, BIP has brought together a library of hard copies of the source materials summarised within it. This library is housed in our offices and is available to BIP members and key stakeholders.

We aim over future years to regularly update both this collection of abstracts document and the library of source materials as new material is added.

We gratefully acknowledge the support of Belfast City Council Good Relations Unit and the Community Relations Council in funding the production of this publication and hope you find this resource relevant and useful.

Chris O'Halloran
Director, Belfast Interface Project.

Introduction

The summer marching season has been a source of tension and disorder for much of the period of political transition in Northern Ireland. Only a relatively small number of parades have proved contentious and been subjected to organised opposition and protests, but the significance of key events in Portadown, Derry Londonderry and parts of Belfast, and the annual cycles of celebration and commemoration, have ensured that tensions have recurred each year.

Parades have been an element of the political culture of the north of Ireland and of the oppositional demands of nationalist and unionists since the eighteenth century. They have also been a recurrent source of tensions and violence. The marching season has repeatedly been a source of conflict at times of tension over the constitutional status of Ireland and, more recently, of Northern Ireland.

Disputes over parades came to the fore in 1995, just a few months after the initial paramilitary ceasefires, but really came to dominate the political agenda following the protests and violence associated with the Drumcree parade in 1996. While parades have long been a source of contention, contemporary disputes can be traced to tensions in Portadown that began in the mid 1980s with the signing of the Anglo-Irish Agreement and concerns among unionists about the future certainty of the union.

This annotated bibliography aims to provide a resource to people wishing to trace and understand the dynamics of current disputes and the various initiatives that have been taken in relation to these.

The bibliography summarises all of the main writings on the current cycle of parades and protests. These include academic studies and documents written by advocates of parading and by their opponents, and also a large number of policy documents that have been generated by the disputes over the past decade. The document includes a number of studies that provide a historical background to parading in Northern Ireland, and also works that focus more on the loyal orders that are responsible for organising the parades.

This bibliography follows an earlier volume on interface issues, and as with that document, this volume will be updated annually with summaries of new materials being made available on the Belfast Interface Project website.

1. **Bell, Desmond (1990)** *Acts of Union: Youth Culture and Sectarianism in Northern Ireland.* **Basingstoke, Macmillan.**

This study is specifically interested in the ways in which youth cultural practices, and particularly marching bands, sustain and reproduce sectarian ethnic identities as a set of shared and learned discourses. Bell uses ethnographic techniques to analyse the rituals of two Protestant marching bands, the Caw Sons of Ulster and Pride of the Valley, to 'deconstruct' unitary notions of Britishness and replace them with a more complex vision of both national and ethnic identity.

Chapter One *Youth Culture and Ethnic Identity* suggests that the lives of young people in Northern Ireland have been shaped by sectarianism and charts the rise in 1970s Northern Ireland of the phenomenon of 'Tartan Gangs'. Bell suggests that there are difficulties applying an interpretive model of youth culture based on an understanding of post-war British youth to Northern Ireland, given that such a model privileges class divisions over ethnic and gender factors. He highlights the role of the civil rights movement in the late 1960s, the 1974 Ulster Workers' Council strike and the 1981 hunger strikes as increasing the street politicisation of young people, with youth cultural practices often sustaining a sectarian 'tradition', and with young people in Northern Ireland becoming the guardians of that tradition. The experiences of Protestant working-class youth are best understood as an attempt to confront and overcome the contradictions experienced within Loyalist parental culture.

Chapter Two *Sons and Daughters of the Gael: Youth in Irish Social Thought* examines the 'youth question' in Ireland, north and south, and highlights how youth subculture has been seen as a threat to cultural tradition. Bell questions the methodology of the correctional character of youth provision in the 1970s which pathologizes youth as at 'risk', and claims that sectarianism should be seen as a political rather than a social problem. Bands and their parades are therefore seen to provide for the dispossessed loyalist youth a sectarian space within which their generational concerns with communal identity and winning public space become infused with the concerns of a parental Loyalist culture with territoriality and ethnic solidarity.

Chapter Three *Situating Sectarianism: Territory, Identity and Empire in Ulster* discusses the historical origins of sectarianism in Ulster linked to the development of a capitalist economy in the nineteenth century. Bell documents loyalist sentiments mainly expressed in traditional Orange marches, which gained their largest followings amongst the Protestant population against the backdrop of the threat of Catholic political advances such as emancipation or Home Rule. The chapter proceeds to examine riots in Derry Londonderry in 1841, 1868, 1870, 1885 and 1899, and contends that this was an era when rigid territorial boundaries were established. Bell notes 'the sectarian territorialization of urban space', and that it is this development that provides the spatial framework within which sectarian youth cultures flourish. The author notes that there is a history of urban youths being centrally involved in ethnically motivated gang conflict in the nineteenth and early twentieth centuries, principally over jobs. He discusses riots in Sandy Row and the Pound area in the 1850s and 1860s, and claims that the role of parades was to maintain group and territorial boundaries.

Chapter Four *Sketches of the Marching Season* provides a brief overview of 'Blood and Thunder' bands. Bell argues that the disappearance of waged work produced a crisis of gender identity for working class teenage males, and these 'Blood and Thunder' bands provide an alternative and increasingly aggressive assertion of masculinity for the marginalized and young working class males. Loyalist street youth culture provides a terrain for young men where traditional male values of bravado and physicality can be rehearsed and paraded.

Ritual parading, graffiti, the painting of kerbstones and so on sustain a symbolic demarcation of the Protestant community and territory at a time when the material base of that community is being eroded. The 'Blood and Thunder' bands also provide a site of resistance to the police, often playing louder at the interfaces, while sectarian abuse serves to sustain communal solidarities as much as to express sectarian hostility. By the mid-1970s the bands had more or less replaced the Tartan Gangs as the focal point around which loyalist youth organised itself. Bell discusses the complex relationship these bands have with the loyalist paramilitaries, with many seeing the bands as an alternative to paramilitary activity, while at the same time many members would be supporters of the various loyalist paramilitaries.

The section charts the evolution of the bands, which started out as 'Kick the Pope' bands, before evolving to become more mature competition orientated bands. There is a tension between older leaders who sought musical discipline and the younger rank and file who are more concerned with the 'craic'. The section provides an overview of two bands, suggesting that they play a key role in cultural reproduction, with the Orange Order trying to restrict them with little success. The bands have now assumed the key role of sustaining a sense of Protestant identity rooted in a particular local territory, with the bandsmen now playing the key part in the ritualised reproduction of a Protestant 'imagined community'.

Chapter Five *Youth and Ghettoization in Northern Ireland* traces the impact of sectarian ghettoization on the lives of young people in Northern Ireland. The chapter suggests the paradox of participants willing to participate in sectarian street violence and yet who at the same time wish to 'get on well' with Catholics. The chapter highlights the sense of restricted mobility felt by many of the young participants, particularly with the Cityside area of Derry Londonderry seen as a 'no-go' area by many young Protestants. Girls appear to be freer in this sense given their marginalisation from the youth sectarian sub-culture. Bell claims that the 'low-achievers' in school are the most vigorous in support of the marching bands and militant loyalism, with seventy percent of those participants in the lowest academic streams in school supporting the bands.

Bell concludes that it is more appropriate to understand the sectarian categorisation of every day life held by many young people in Northern Ireland in terms of the influence of peer-group association and youth cultural practices rather than reference to a clinical theory of individual pathology or overtly deterministic theory of generational cultural transmission. Sectarianism and racism must be understood as coming from a youth-cultural response in specific material situations as opposed to personal prejudice, and by the late 1980s it is the marching bands with their expressive display of Protestant identity and difference that have become the most important mobilizing agency for Protestant working class youth.

Chapter Six *Economic Marginalization and Blocked Inheritance* assesses the impact of mass unemployment in Northern Ireland leading to young people now exploring alternative codes of cultural inheritance and communal heritage no longer dependent upon the labour market. The chapter suggests that many sections of the Protestant population and especially the working-class found it harder to make a collective readjustment to 'hard times' than their Catholic neighbours. Bell claims that statistics show a virtual collapse of employment possibilities for the contemporary school leaver in the Derry Londonderry area, with only an estimated ten percent of males in full-time work. Bell argues that it is in this context of economic marginalization faced by Protestant working-class young people that youthful sectarianism can be charted.

The final chapter *Postscript on Practice* implicates British Imperialism as responsible for sectarianism in Northern Ireland, and alleges that sectarianism in Northern Ireland achieves its exclusivist effects through cultural practices of territorial demarcation and communal identification. Bell is critical of approaches to tackle sectarianism which focus explicitly on education, rather arguing for the need for a more imaginative approach to the secondary curriculum in which young people need to be encouraged to critically examine their own cultural tradition. He concludes that Orange popular culture, whilst fostering a degree of hostility towards Catholics, also functions to encourage local loyalties, and provide public and recreational space and the symbolic resources for the construction by the young of a distinctively Protestant sense of community for an increasingly beleaguered people.

2. British-Irish Inter-Parliamentary Body (2001) *The Cultural Significance of Parades.* Available at http://www.biipb.org/biipb/committee/commd/8102.htm

This report focuses on the broader significance of parades and emphasises the motives of the participants within parades in both Northern Ireland and Scotland. The paper opens by discussing the historical background to the major parading organisations in Northern Ireland, and notes that there was sectarian violence throughout most of the nineteenth century, with parades often actively discouraged by the government. A summary of evidence is provided and the concept of tradition is examined. The report highlights that the parading organisations that talked to the Committee argued that they marched to celebrate tradition and culture and not to antagonise others. The view of tradition in Scotland was seen as less localised than in Northern Ireland, and although there were reported to be traditional routes in Scotland, most participants were concerned not to cause offence and often voluntarily rerouted their parades. The situation in Scotland is seen as very different, as both the Orange Order and the Ancient Order of Hibernians had no problem in changing 'traditional' routes where they were not welcome.

Parade participants are seen as having a variety of motives for taking part, including religious, political and social motives, and the report draws on Jarman and Bryan's argument that this diversity in motives in Northern Ireland reflects the fragmentation which has occurred within Unionism over the past thirty years. In Scotland, the British-Irish Inter-Parliamentary Body assert that the 'struggle for respectability' seems to have been won, and they explore both the positive and negative impacts that parades in both Northern Ireland and Scotland can have on the community as a whole. In positive terms, the social role of the Orders is highlighted, while more negatively parades are seen as having damaged local economies.

Women in the Orders are seen as occupying a 'semi-detached' position, and the publication moves on to focus specifically on two areas of contention surrounding parades, the Ancient Order of Hibernians (AOH) parade in Kilkeel and the Apprentice Boys march in Derry Londonderry. The Derry

Londonderry example is discussed from 1995 onwards, and is cited as a relative success for mediation, although 'feeder' parades such as those that have taken place on the Lower Ormeau Road are seen as more problematic.

The report concludes that the media have an important role to play in reducing public ignorance of the role of parades in the cultural and social life of their communities. Parades combine different elements: a sense of community, religion and history. The report contends that it is the responsibility of the Orders in Ireland to replicate Scotland and ensure that those with paramilitary links do not hijack 'traditional' parades. The authors assert that the perception of tradition can diverge from the reality of social change. This is seen to particularly be the case with 'feeder' parades, when the argument of tradition is much less clear. The British-Irish Inter-Parliamentary Body state that there needs to be sensitivity on all sides and full engagement with the Parades Commission, and if this is the case then parades can perhaps become an accepted part of the social fabric of Northern Ireland.

3. **Bryan, Dominic (1998) Ireland's Very Own Jurassic Park: The Mass Media, Orange Parades and the Discourse on Tradition. In Buckley, Anthony D. (ed.) *Symbols in Northern Ireland*. Belfast, Institute of Irish Studies.**

Bryan examines how the media have tended to cover Orange parades, he argues that newspapers and broadcasters depict the parades as governed by history and understand them as simply part of 'tradition', ignoring the contemporary aspects of parades. Bryan sees claims of tradition as legitimation for a political position against change, and he is not surprised that the loyalist community claim a 'right to march' along 'traditional' routes given the mass media's constant referrals to the longevity of the events, and the use of terms such as 'tradition' and 'heritage'.

The chapter discusses the Twelfth of July parade, highlighting the paradox in a symbolic, repetitive structure formalised as 'tradition' with the dynamic changes that have occurred over time. The author discusses how this is played out in the mass media coverage of the Twelfth as far back as 1738, when the News Letter, although generally supportive of the marchers, was critical of sectarian clashes. By the 1870s much of this criticism had waned in the face of Irish nationalist opposition, and throughout the Stormont years Bryan asserts that each year the success of Northern Ireland as a state was reported in terms of the reported turnout at the annual parades. The emphasis was to maintain unity, and newspaper headlines show as little sign of division as possible. The overwhelming media discourse is one of 'tradition' and of an occasion which has been passed down through the generations.

Bryan contends that it is significant that signs of the consumption of alcohol or the presence of paramilitary symbols are not shown, rather the image of continuity and historical stability is shown, and there is a media focus on the 'respectable' Orangemen rather than the 'Blood and Thunder' bands. In contrast, national and foreign media tend to use more aggressive, threatening and sectarian images of the parades. The chapter concludes that media discourse ignores the changes taking place, and that there are two different perceptions of the Twelfth, one as a festival, the other as a territorial, drunken and sectarian occasion. Bryan notes that both of these images accept the historical and traditional foundations of the events, even critiques from Irish nationalists on the Twelfth itself.

4. Bryan, Dominic (1999) The Right to March: Parading a Loyal Protestant Identity in Northern Ireland. In Allen, Tim and Eade, John (eds.) *Divided Europeans: Understanding Ethnicities in Conflict.* **The Hague, Kluwer Law International.**

This chapter discusses parades disputes over Orangemen's 'right to march' in the context of the disturbances at Drumcree in 1996. Bryan outlines Orange parades as ritual events that define the ethnic boundaries between the two communities, and attempts to explain why these parades are so important and the role they play in the relationships between Catholic and Protestant communities and Protestant communities and the state.

The chapter examines the historical relationship between Orange parades and Protestant ethnicity and Bryan contends that the appearance of consensus provided by the parades disguises a more complex reality in which the Protestant community is rife with political divisions. The role of the Orange Order historically is seen as one that can unify diverse Protestant denominations and economic interests in opposition to Irish nationalism. Bryan describes how the relationship between the Orange Institution and the state changed through the eighteenth century, and notes that there have been frequent attempts to ban or reroute marches historically. The chapter argues that at present parades give the appearance of timeless events, but have been actively contested and changed over time.

The chapter explains why parades in Portadown have become the focus of the conflict surrounding parades, outlining that sectarian confrontations accompanying parades have a long history in Portadown. Between 1873 and 1892 there were numerous serious disturbances and during the 1970s trouble flared up again at a time when elements of the parade had changed to include more raucous 'Blood and Thunder' bands. Despite relatively quiet years until the early 1990s, Bryan notes that in 1992 parading became high profile again with the nationalist protests on the Lower Ormeau Road, while the paramilitary ceasefires of 1994 allowed nationalist groups to be more forthright in their opposition to contentious parades. The chapter describes events at Drumcree in 1995 and claims that the 'right to parade' was symbolic of the relationship between the two ethnic groups and the state. Throughout the events of the summers of 1995 and 1996, political figures followed certain strategies to maximise their political capital as 'defenders' of their community.

Bryan analyses how Orange parades have developed as part of a Protestant ethnic identity and states that the parades in themselves are not in any simple sense expressions of Protestant hegemony, but rather are part of a more complex set of relationships within the Protestant community and between that group and the state. Bryan argues that Orange parades are an attempt to give the appearance of unity and to legitimate the present with the past, and that the concept of 'tradition' ignores the important changes that have taken place within parades, including the increase in the number and role of 'Blood and Thunder' bands and the carrying of paramilitary symbols. These major divisions within unionism are to some extent played out during parades, and Bryan asserts that the ritual displays of Orangeism play a complex role at the intersection between the law enforcement arm of the state and the relationship between the two communities.

5. **Bryan, Dominic (2000)** *Orange Parades: The Politics of Ritual and Control.* **London, Pluto Press.**

This book tries to explain why Orange parades are such a prominent issue and how rituals have come to be utilised as a political resource. Bryan suggests that the ritual commemorations and symbols of Orangeism have played a far more complex and dynamic role in Irish politics than is generally assumed, suggesting that the Twelfth should be seen as a dynamic political ritual as opposed to a discourse of 'tradition'.

Chapter One: *Drumcree an Introduction to Parade Disputes* discusses the notion of 'respectable' Orangeism after the 1870s which is used by the powerful to buttress their power, with middle-class and capital-owning Protestants finding Orangeism and parades a useful, and yet an awkward and dangerous resource in retaining power.

Chapter Two: *Northern Ireland: Ethnicity, Politics and Ritual* contends that the civil rights demonstrations in the late 1960s challenged the unionist political status quo and raised questions of political identity and power. The chapter examines the complex and developing relationships between classes, between ethnic groups and between the state and those ethnic communities. Bryan outlines that the most common forms of ritual in Northern Ireland are commemorative events, and that the history of Orangeism is one in which elites used parades to try to control autonomous social action, with the concept of tradition tending to be invoked in times of change when people's social relationships are being undermined.

Chapter Three: *Appropriating William and Inventing the Twelfth* is an attempt to place Orange parades in historical context. This chapter explores the invention of the Twelfth and then its appropriation by particular class interests in the second half of the nineteenth century. Bryan argues that although Williamite rituals and commemorations existed prior to the formation of the Orange Order, they did not attain widespread appeal until after the formation of the Orange Order in 1795. This formation helped to codify and control the Boyne commemorations more formally. The author asserts that gaining and maintaining respectability in the face of public disorder has been a problem for the Orange Order since its inception, as the Order owed its development to lower-class sectarian confrontations that put at risk the economic and political stability of the country. Bryan points out that 1795 to 1870 was a turbulent period for the Order and the chapter documents various parades disturbances during this period, particularly between 1830 and 1835, with July 1857 seeing some of the worst rioting on record. These riots occurred against a backdrop of constant efforts to stop parades during this period.

Chapter Four: *Parading 'Respectable' Politics* examines the appeal of William Johnson and the increasing respectability of parades as events at which local politicians would find it necessary to speak and be seen at, a phenomenon which came to dominate Orangeism for the next 100 years. It is in this period that the author suggests that we see a change in the relationship between the Orange Institution, conservative politics and the growing working class of Belfast. The 1872 to 1886 era saw the first home rule bill, leading to the Twelfth becoming a more highly controlled and politicised event. Bryan argues that the impact of a number of factors including the formation of the Ulster Volunteer Force (UVF) against the backdrop of a third home rule bill, their blood sacrifice at the Somme and the aftermath of the 1916 Easter Rising led to the Orange Institution more than doubling its membership from 8,834 to 18,800 during this time. The chapter concludes that the fifty years between 1870-1920 saw the Orange Institution develop from a relatively localised, rural and politically marginal organisation to one that dominated the political and economic structures of the urbanising north of Ireland. It was utilised by land and industrial owning classes to create an identity in which unionism could develop in opposition to Home Rule.

Chapter Five: *Rituals of State* outlines that between 1921 and 1971 the Orange Institution had a position of great political power, with 122 of 760 seats on the Ulster Unionist Council. All of Northern Ireland's Prime Ministers were Orangemen, and all but three members of the cabinet between 1921-1969 were Orangemen. The author claims that the Twelfth parades became rituals of state. The development of nationalist and Catholic and unionist and Protestant parading 'traditions' were closely related to their power within the Northern State. The post-war Twelfth is often remembered as a relaxed, good-humoured time, which gave precedence to religion over politics, but Bryan highlights the role of Ian Paisley and internal wranglings within the UUP as leading to the Twelfth becoming an arena through which political forces could play out their relationships. Although the 1950s were remembered as a 'golden era' for Orangeism, closer analysis reveals some of the frictions within Orangeism that were to become more obvious by the mid-1960s.

Chapter Six: *'You Can March – Can Others?'* discusses the questioning of the hegemonic position of Orangeism from the mid-1960s onwards by the civil rights movement, nationalists, socialists, republicans and the British state. The middle class also were no longer overtly attracted to Orangeism and there were disturbances almost every year from 1965-1977 during the marching season. The fall of the Stormont regime and return to Direct Rule are discussed at length and the book argues that the Twelfth changed from being an expression of the state of Northern Ireland and its Unionist government to an event organised by an increasingly divided and disillusioned unionist community for its own defence. There was anger in working class unionist areas with the failure of the unionist elite to deal with the Irish Republican Army, which led to a rise in 'Blood and Thunder' or 'Kick the Pope' bands. Bryan therefore suggests that the Twelfth became a site for political struggle, and he believes that in some sense the Twelfth was losing its respectability.

Chapter Seven: *The Orange and Other Loyal Orders* aims to understand the role that the Orange Institution plays in the modern politics of Northern Ireland and the significance of specific parades. Its present structure and membership is examined, as is its ideological purpose, and the section also documents the qualifications required to be an Orangeman. The chapter highlights the historic link between the Orange Institution and the Ulster Unionist party, and discusses the practical advantages of being an Orangeman. There is also a brief synopsis of the roles of the Royal Black Institution, the Royal Arch Purple, the Apprentice Boys and the Independent Orange Order.

Chapter Eight: *The Marching Season* emphasises the importance of locality and geography to parades, suggesting that the class and ethnic make-up of the local area affects parades. It outlines a typology of nine different parades, and discusses the nature of the 'Blood and Thunder bands'. Bryan argues that they have been the most distinctive development in loyalist political culture since the 1960s, and that their use of paramilitary insignia has been problematic for 'respectable' Orangeism, particularly since almost all of the bands have no direct connection with the Order.

Chapter Nine: *The Twelfth* provides a generalised description of the Twelfth and aims to provide an understanding of the event itself, its apparent contradictions, its nuances, moments of conflict and above all its political dynamics. The role of bass-drumming as a marker of masculinity is highlighted, particularly at a time when there was high urban unemployment and low-skilled work reduced the ability of males to assert themselves.

Chapter Ten: *'Tradition', Control and Resistance* looks at how recent shifts in political power have influenced parades and how the claim of 'tradition' is used to maintain the legitimacy of the events. Bryan explores the way that parades and discourses surrounding them have been formed and controlled since the 1970s, and analyses in particular the way in which the changing relationship between the state and Protestant community has been reflected in 'Blood and Thunder' bands, and consequent attempts by the Orange Institution to keep control of parades.

The author asserts that from 1795 to the 1870s Orangeism and its ritual expressions were predominantly lower-class phenomena which were both utilised and abandoned by the state at different times depending upon prevailing political conditions. After 1920, the Twelfth became a ritual of state, more 'respectable' and less overtly threatening than previously. After 1972, working-class loyalism became more assertive and the Twelfth became a sub-culture of resistance to the forces of the state. This era saw more criticism of senior Orangemen at parades, an increase in the flying of Northern Ireland flags in unionist/loyalist areas, an increase in the number of parades and bands, and an increasingly strained relationship between unionists and the Royal Ulster Constabulary. The Twelfth became a site of resistance to the state and from the 1960s onwards there was a more militant form of sectarianism developing in fractured working-class areas. The parades between 1977 and 1980 were more peaceful affairs, but after the 1981 hunger strikes, unionism felt threatened and 'respectable' unionism was in retreat. The chapter discusses the increasing difficulties with parades as the 1990s progressed, and particularly in 1995 at Drumcree when the political fractures within Orangeism became clear.

Chapter Eleven: *Return to Drumcree* suggests that Drumcree in 1998 may well prove to be a defining act for the Institution due to the introduction of the Public Processions (Northern Ireland) Act and the Parades Commission. It is claimed that the problem for the Orange Order in organising mass events meant that they were allowing a range of interest to mobilise and utilise the protest, including loyalist paramilitaries.

6. **Bryan, Dominic (2000) Drumcree and 'The Right to March':** **Orangeism, Ritual and Politics in Northern Ireland. In Fraser, T.G.** **(ed.) *The Irish Parading Tradition: Following the Drum.* Basingstoke,** **Macmillan.**

The chapter begins by outlining Ian Paisley's suggestion that the future of Northern Ireland lay in the right of members of the Orange Order to parade back from their annual Boyne commemorative church service along the Garvaghy Road, which Bryan suggests may date from 1807 or even previously. It explores the political dynamics of events-rituals and examines the relations between those events and the state, and within the nationalist community in an attempt to better understand the Drumcree dispute.

The 1860s and 1870s saw regular efforts by Protestant drumming parties to assert themselves by marching through the predominantly Catholic Tunnel area of Portadown, while most nationalist attempts at parades were attacked, such as the Lady's Day parade in 1872. The author contends that this is due to the fact that, in historical periods when Irish nationalism was organised and prepared to assert itself, disputes over parades were liable to become more frequent. During the Troubles, Orange parades became more assertive and confrontational, and any attempts to stop them were seen by unionists as a challenge to British sovereignty.

Bryan outlines historical state concern with Orangeism, and notes the history of problems associated with parading in Portadown. After the introduction of Direct Rule in 1972, the Order moved from being closely tied to the institutions of state to being an interest group struggling to maintain a position of respect and power. He uses the example of the Ulster Defence Association (UDA) offering the Orangemen protection to parade through the Tunnel area in 1972 as illustrating how the Institution was beginning to move away from the state and notions of respectability.

7. **Bryan, Dominic (2005) Fanatics, Mobs and Terrorists: The Dynamics of Orange Parades in Northern Ireland. In Hughes, Matthew, and Johnson, Gaynor (eds.) *Fanaticism and Conflict in the Modern Age.* London, Frank Cass.**

This chapter argues that the events of 9/11 changed the political make up of the world by creating the ideological space for simplistic categorisations of divisions to occur, and allowed a claim that terrorists are illegitimate, fanatical and often religious. Bryan discusses this in the context of the dispute over the Drumcree church parade from 1995 onwards, and questions whether or not Northern Ireland in the month of July is the place to look for fanatics.

He briefly describes the events at Drumcree in 1995 and highlights the contradiction in people professing loyalty to the state and security forces at the same time as attacking the police. The chapter notes that although some define this violent behaviour as mad and illogical, many 'respectable' people took part as they were driven by a belief in certain values strongly held within their community. The author attempts to understand the context in which the events of Drumcree have taken place and considers three main factors. Firstly, that Orange parades are central symbolically to the identity of unionists and an attack on a parade is seen as an attack upon a British, Protestant way of life. Secondly, as Drumcree is perceived by many within the unionist community as a 'traditional' parade it holds a special significance. Bryan asserts that a 'traditional' ritual is important as it legitimises a political position. Thirdly, the context of the commemorations is important in displaying a sense of ethnic territory and mapping out of space. These factors, together with the fact that Portadown has a special significance and is known as the 'Orange Citadel', make the Drumcree parade somewhat different from other contentious parades. The author concludes that Northern Ireland since the late 1960s has been the site of many actions that could easily be described as fanatical, but to resort to such descriptions leads us no nearer to understanding the actions of people who are not clinically ill. The concept of the fanatic is said to be not sociologically useful as a description of behaviour.

Bryan draws comparisons between the jubilant scenes of Ian Paisley and David Trimble holding their arms aloft in 1995 with the role of the Ulster

Defence Association, the Democratic Unionist Party and the Ulster Unionist Party in 1986 in competing for the control of Orangeism. He argues that the 1996 confrontations acted as a rallying point for the UUP and DUP at a time when divisions were developing over a peace process strategy. Despite this, Bryan believes that the Orange Order relied on tactics which they could not control in the end, and which led to strained relations with many others within the Protestant community. The chapter proposes that the Order in supporting the hard-line stance of Portadown district had to pay the costs elsewhere, and alleges that the parades dispute provided the republican movement with useful forms of community mobilisation.

Bryan concludes that the power of the Orange Order from the 1870s to the 1970s began to wane, and Drumcree provided a moment of apparent unity, which as a by-product also helped to get David Trimble elected as leader of the UUP. Drumcree highlighted the importance of Portadown disputes in illustrating the changing politics in Northern Ireland.

8. **Bryan, Dominic (2006) 'Traditional' Parades, Conflict and Change: Orange Parades and Other Rituals in Northern Ireland, 1960-2000. In Neuheiser, Jorg and Schaich, Michael (eds.) *Political Rituals in Great Britain: 1700-2000*. Augsburg, Wisner-Verlag.**

In this chapter, Bryan explores the role of rituals and the discourse of 'tradition' in the Northern Ireland conflict. The paper looks at the role of public political ritual during a period of conflict in Northern Ireland between 1960 and 2000 and argues that public events during this era were central to what took place. Bryan suggests that it is precisely at a period of time when a society is undertaking change that ritual events can provide a mechanism whereby apparent continuity is being maintained. It is suggested that the greater the claims to tradition, the greater the likelihood of finding fundamental changes in the tradition.

The author claims that it was the inability of the Northern Ireland government to deal with the public rituals that directly led to the communal violence which preceded the 1970s paramilitary violence. As the peace process developed in the 1990s, public rituals returned to the fore. Orange Order rituals are viewed as being part of the formation of sectarian space in both rural and urban areas of the north of Ireland, and Bryan believes that Orange parades provided a ritual through which public space was dominated, noting that even until the 1930s new 'traditional' routes were being added to increase the numbers of parades.

The consequence of the outbreak of the Troubles for the Orange Order and Orange parades was dramatic, and as traditional boundaries became more clearly demarcated, some traditional routes taken by Orangemen began to look more like invasions of territory. Bryan notes that a 1970 Northern Ireland Office report highlighted that there were an 'unreasonable number of processions' and it also suggested that Orange parades should be stopped on the Grosvenor, Saintfield and Crumlin Roads and parts of the Antrim Road.

The symbolic content of Orange parades has changed since the 1960s, with an increasing number of 'Blood and Thunder' bands, new parades, new flags and other developments. Bryan believes that the key to understanding these changes is to examine the networks of political power and influence within which the Orange Order has worked. Some of the changes in the parades reflected the fact that many loyalists in working-class Belfast looked to the paramilitaries for defence, and the Twelfth started to reflect this through the development of the 'Blood and Thunder' bands, an increase in paramilitary flags and so on. The author claims that the parading tradition was directly reflecting fundamental changes in power and communal politics within the Protestant community in the 1970s and 1980s, and the ritual parades are seen as providing a space within which a variety of often contradictory political expressions appear. Orange parades were adapting to changing social and political circumstances.

The chapter traces the origins of the contemporary dispute over Drumcree to events in 1985 and 1986 particularly in Portadown, and documents restrictions on Orange Order routes in the 1990s in a number of areas. This period saw a significant alteration in the position of traditional Orange rituals and public space, and although the Order have kept a discourse that they must maintain their 'traditional' parades, Bryan utilises Bourdieu's theory of orthodoxy to suggest that when discourses of heterodoxy oppose the dominant ideas, invariably tradition will be invoked as an argument of orthodoxy. The author concludes that the civil rights marches of the late 1960s threatened the status quo and Orange parades have attempted to maintain their importance through public space. These rituals were often a site of contest within Unionism and the parades reflected changes in unionist and loyalist politics, the decline of the Ulster Unionist Party and corresponding increase in Democratic Unionist Party support, and the rise of loyalist paramilitaries.

9. **Bryan, Dominic; Fraser, T.G; and Dunn, Seamus (1995)** *Political Rituals: Loyalist Parades in Portadown.* **Coleraine, Centre for the Study of Conflict.**

The stated brief of this project is to place and investigate parades in the political, religious, social and cultural life of Northern Ireland. The authors also seek to examine the controversy surrounding the concept of 'tradition'. One key aspect to be investigated is the relationship between parades and periods of particular crisis or anxiety for the Ulster Protestant community. This report examines some of the details of the local conflict in Portadown over the two years of 1985/86 with the two main areas of contention in Portadown being the Tunnel / Obins Street and the Garvaghy Road. The research documents six major riots and numerous other incidents during this period, and places them within their broader historical and political context, particularly since relations between Protestants and the police and between both communities worsened against the backdrop of the signing of the Anglo-Irish Agreement in November 1985. The research is predominantly based on newspaper reports, which allows for an analysis of the role of the media in fashioning perceptions and in constructing and reconstructing the meanings of those events. Bryan et al review some of the ways in which rituals are examined, provide an overview of Portadown's history and geography from the 1950s, and speculate on some possible resolutions to the parades issue.

It is outlined that Portadown has been closely linked to the Orange Order since its formation, and that sectarian confrontation accompanying parades has a long history in Portadown and is often connected to commemorative periods. In the Tunnel area, there has been a history of problems from 1873, and for much of the later nineteenth century the Tunnel area required heavy policing during the month of July. The onset of the Troubles saw difficulties come to be associated with parades again and the report lists incidents as occurring from the late 1960s through the 1970s. The case of Portadown is said to be interesting given that it contains a mixture of urban and rural parade characteristics, with both 'Blood and Thunder' bands and more middle class silver and pipe bands.

The publication notes the increased tension associated with the hunger strikes of 1981 and cites the rerouting of the St. Patrick's Day Parade of 1985 as the start of the modern day dispute over parade routes. The booklet assesses the political ramifications of ongoing developments during 1985 and 1986, while disputes over rerouting and banning continued in August and September 1985. The debate over parades and the relationship between the police and the population of Portadown led to the town becoming symbolic of the parading dispute in general.

The authors examine the impact of the signing of the Anglo-Irish Agreement in 1985. On Easter Monday 1 April 1986, the banning of the parade led to violence with one man killed and fifty people injured in the disturbances. The authors describe the situation in the build up to the 1986 summer marching season and during the Drumcree church parade in July 1986, in which the police were under attack from both unionists and nationalists. Unionists in particular believed that the police were being used as an arm of the Anglo-Irish Agreement. Other areas of Northern Ireland experienced trouble as the Twelfth concentrated resentment against the Anglo-Irish Agreement. The booklet notes that 1986 saw the introduction of a band contract, and a United Ulster Bands Association was established. Although the period between 1987 and 1994 is described as still oppositional to parades, heavy policing limited the violence. Since 1987, the Drumcree march has abandoned the Tunnel area along Obins street and instead has been rerouted along the Garvaghy Road as it was believed this route would be easier to police.

The report states that there was a diverse range of parties seeking to utilise the parading 'tradition' in a rapidly changing political context. After 1972, many groups within the parades themselves became 'dissenters', and began using rituals that had been conservative celebrations of the status quo as a means of voicing their opposition. This led to the increase in the presence of 'Blood and Thunder' bands within the parades. At a time of increased alienation for Protestants, these bands could express dissatisfaction with the state and the police. Bryan et al argue that control of the parade is therefore contested amongst groups such as the UUP, DUP, UDA, and suggest that it is perhaps at those times when senior Orangemen have lost influence over the ritual events that they are likely to resort to an appeal to 'tradition' as a means to reassert control. The report contends that the lasting effects of events in Portadown have been a change in the relationship between the police and the Protestant community and shifting perceptions of the police which turned the RUC into an 'outgroup' in the eyes of significant numbers of Protestants.

The document suggests that the situation as it stands in 1995 is emblematic of the wider political problem. It contends that an identity will need to be created which is of greater inclusiveness, with a need to extend notions of 'Irishness' and 'Britishness'. Despite the rhetorical use of the term 'tradition', Bryan et al assert that the parades have not remained the same, but have changed over the years both in content and meaning. If Orangemen were to walk quietly as a religious institution playing hymns in nationalist areas, it is argued that it would be harder to see any valid argument for keeping them out. The report concludes however, that without a broader political settlement the situation with regards to parades disputes is unlikely to change.

10. Bryan, Dominic and Jarman, Neil (1997) **Parading Tradition, Protesting Triumphalism: Utilising Anthropology in Public Policy.** In Donnan, Hastings and McFarlane, Graham (eds.) *Culture and Policy in Northern Ireland: Anthropology in the Public Arena.* Belfast, Institute of Irish Studies.

Bryan and Jarman in this chapter outline that Drumcree in 1996 was one of over fifty parade disputes in that year, the vast majority of which involved the rights of Protestant organisations to hold 'traditional' parades through or near to Catholic communities. One crucial element in the development of a parading 'tradition' in Ireland was the relationship which those parading had with the state. In the 1790s, Orange parades were encouraged by the state, but by the middle of the nineteenth century the frequent sectarian clashes which accompanied them resulted in heavy policing and often the banning of parades. The authors suggest that it was only in the late nineteenth century that Orange parades gained respectability among the middle and upper classes.

By the 1980s parades were once again going through political changes. In particular, unionists saw the 1985 Anglo-Irish Agreement as a threat and this combined with other factors such as the increasingly aggressive RUC policing of Orange parades led to disturbances in Portadown in 1985. For unionists, the blocking or rerouting of parades showed a tangible loss of their power. Disturbances in 1996 seriously damaged already fragile community relations and heightened the growing perception that the police and government gave in to threats of loyalist violence. Bryan and Jarman argue that two positions characterise the debate: one position focusing on the tradition of parades and the other focusing on the need for the consent of the local community for a parade to pass through an area.

The authors outline a perception within the Catholic community that all Orange parades are triumphalist and that this ignores the internal differences between church and feeder parades, rural and urban differences, and so on. The chapter moves on to outline a typology of nine different parade types and comments that the different types of parade reflect different elements of unionism and Protestant identity and changing political and social circumstances. Most disputes occur at the smaller, local parades and there tends to be more resistance by unionists at attempts to reroute church parades, while efforts to reroute the Drumcree parade are seen as an attack on Protestantism itself in a way that the rerouting of a mini-Twelfth is not. The authors conclude that the marching season is a complex series of dynamic events in which nationalist residents and the Loyal Orders often misinterpret each other's actions. According to the authors, parades are often correctly perceived as both religious and triumphalist, and the section finishes with an exploration of how people felt the parades impasse could be resolved, proposing seven different options for a possible resolution.

11. **Bryan, Dominic and Jarman, Neil (1999)** *Independent Intervention: Monitoring the Police, Parades and Public Order.* **Belfast, Democratic Dialogue.**

The report looks at the role played by members of civil society in the numerous disputes over contentious parades and focuses on the work of human rights groups, community based activists and stewards. It is primarily based on observation conducted at parades and interviews with people involved in monitoring. The work attempts to unravel the complexities of monitoring groups and the diversity of their approaches, aims and practices.

Chapter One *Introduction* begins by outlining that disputes over the right to parade have brought public order issues to the fore in Northern Ireland, and have threatened to undermine political progress. Parades are seen as particularly significant at times of political transition; since the paramilitary ceasefires of 1994 it has been easier to forge new alliances, and parades have been a site for political confrontation. The chapter asserts that the presence of a number of monitors has contributed to a more peaceful range of protests in the past two years.

Chapter Two *What is a Monitor?* establishes some theoretical concepts and explores approaches to monitoring. Monitors are identified as those people, groups, or NGOs who are third-parties to a dispute and who aim to observe and record what is taking place. Despite this apparent reactive role, Jarman and Bryan claim that monitors can also have a more active role. The chapter offers a loose typology of those involved at parades disputes and asserts that a diverse range of bodies undertake monitoring, including the police, participants, stewards and political representatives among others. The groups are discussed in turn with reference to their degree of intervention, independence, privileges and perceptions and their relations of power. Some differentiation is made between groups who act at an event itself and others who are more concerned with the long-term picture.

One factor which distinguishes monitors from other groups is an element of independence; however this is not the same as being neutral. The chapter assesses the difficulties of raising suspicion about one's role by being seen moving between protagonists and highlights that relations of power are vital in understanding the role of the monitor. The chapter further contends that all observations are always partial, as an incident can look quite different to two different people. The chapter concludes that the boundaries between different monitors are not always clearly defined and that if a role is shifted from one to another there can be problems in returning to the original role, and this may hinder their ability to monitor in the future.

Chapter Three *International Approaches to Monitoring* looks at forms of monitoring carried out by international organisations such as the United Nations, the European Union, the Organisation for Security and Cooperation in Europe and others, and focuses on the role played by foreign monitors in verifying the fairness of the election process in other countries. The chapter then discusses four recent examples of independent indigenous monitoring in England, the USA and South Africa. The authors provide an overview of monitoring requirements such as that required under the OSCE handbook and Code of Conduct. Despite international monitors only being supposed to observe events, in practice some situations required a more interventionist stance. The chapter provides some criticisms of international monitoring missions, including their motives and often lack of local knowledge, and then proceeds to discuss the growth in local monitoring groups in many countries. The authors note some of the positive factors of using local monitors, including their better local knowledge, but highlight that there will always be a questioning of their neutrality and impartiality.

The report documents that monitoring was seen as active and facilitating the process in South Africa and helped to increase the credibility of the process. The section highlights the role that African National Congress (ANC) and Inkatha Freedom Party (IFP) members had as activists. As key political members they were organised into monitoring teams, yet the code of conduct required them to take a neutral position. The success in this project was that the political activists came to be seen less as party members than as peace accord monitors. Their role included active liaison with the police and sometimes they advised the police to withdraw from areas to decrease tension. Jarman and Bryan identify this as a three-tiered problem solving structure with the stewards the first to deal with a problem; if they fail then the monitors try, and if they fail only then do the security forces become involved. This gives a greater opportunity for a peaceful resolution. This organised independent monitoring was a feature of the civil response to escalating violence at demonstrations during periods of tension, but the teams largely came to an end after the 1994 elections. The chapter concludes by highlighting the differences in approaches in three main areas:

the orientation of observation and who they focus on; the level of intervention favoured, and any positioning in favour of one party. The authors assert that this has led to four practical approaches to monitoring public events: observer monitors, partisan monitors, reactive monitors and interventionist monitors.

Chapter Four *Monitoring in Northern Ireland* reviews the attempts made to monitor violence and public order disputes before the ceasefires. The roles of two groups are briefly examined, the Central Citizens Defence Committee which was a non-violent body monitoring relations between the Catholic community and the Army/RUC in the late 1960s, and INNATE (Irish Network for Non-violent Action Training and Education). INNATE involved twenty groups developing models and training for monitors and organised observer teams on the Garvaghy Road between 1988 and 1993, and their use in the early 1990s was facilitated by a drop in violence with observers once again becoming viable. Jarman and Bryan contend that the presence of independent observers can lead to more objective recording and influence sides to be on their 'best behaviour'.

Chapter Five *Monitoring Human Rights* distinguishes between two different types of human rights groups: human-rights groups and solidarity monitors. It provides some background to the Committee for the Administration of Justice, Human Rights Watch and Amnesty International who each attempt to subject the policing of public disorder to an independent form of accountability. This is contrasted with solidarity groups such as the Irish Emergency Parades Committee, who have an allegiance with one group alone. Jarman and Bryan argue that the solidarity approach taken by such groups with the nationalist community in many cases reduces their effectiveness.

Chapter Six *Monitoring Public Order* documents groups that take an active role in helping ensure peaceful outcomes at parades. These mediators include religious leaders and members of community relations and reconciliation groups. Mediators have a different role than the monitors in that they intervene if needed and do not see their role as influencing wider public opinion. The chapter provides a brief review of four community based initiatives involving the Community Development Centre in North Belfast, Peace and Reconciliation Group, Women Together / Independent Observer Network and the Meath Peace Group. Jarman and Bryan state that these initiatives had some commonalities including a willingness to intervene on the ground, a persuasion role, intervening with one party, and providing community based monitors who are not necessarily independent, but who use their stature within the community and function differently to observers.

Chapter Seven *Stewarding Public Events* defines stewarding as an attempt by organisers to manage an event by controlling those attending. The steward's ability to act is based on legitimacy, with Jarman and Bryan alleging that stewarding fulfils two interrelated purposes: internal control and fulfilling external obligations. The former of these is connected to the conveyance of messages while the latter is in regards to health and safety legislation and social responsibility. Good stewarding should mean that there is less need for highly visible policing. Jarman and Bryan outline the contrasting practice of stewarding in Northern Ireland, as the nationalist community has developed extensive crowd management arrangements whereas the Loyal Orders have largely relied on the RUC. The quality of stewarding varies considerably, and the report assesses the Apprentice Boys of Derry and their steward-training project.

Jarman and Bryan argue that the first part of a solution to safety concerns regarding public events in Northern Ireland is good stewarding. They state that a significant aspect to the dispute in Derry Londonderry has been the anti-social behaviour of some within the parade due to the influence of alcohol and the hostility of some outsiders. Improved stewarding in 1998 did make a difference, with liaison and planning between police and organisations greatly improved. The chapter concludes that stewarding needs to move away from its current ad-hoc approach.

Chapter Eight *Future Monitoring* concentrates on three forms of monitoring: human rights monitors, community based monitors, and stewards, with each group having a specific relationship with formal policing structures. The 1970s and 1980s violence resulted in limited possibilities to use monitors, and the ceasefires created the space for peaceful protest and developed a sense of safety. The chapter examines the role that civil society can play in supporting moves towards a peaceful and democratic society. The Human Rights Commission, it is claimed, should develop a particular interest in the activities of monitors, and in particular human rights, while the Parades Commission should build better relationships with independent monitoring groups.

Jarman and Bryan suggest that the experience elsewhere highlights the powerful role observers and monitors can play if they remain independent, and assert that human rights monitoring in the future could provide an official policing oversight function and the Human Rights Commission could use monitors to evaluate specific human rights abuses. Community based monitoring has been successful in Belfast and Derry Londonderry, but has only really worked where significant community development work had already been undertaken. The publication concludes that a formal definition of stewarding standards is needed and that a recognised training scheme should improve the standard of stewarding.

12. Bryett, Keith (1997) Does Drumcree '96 Tell Us Anything about the RUC? *Critical Criminology*, Volume 8, Number 1.

This essay identifies some of the potential consequences of policing Drumcree for the RUC's public image, and compares these potential perceptions of police performance with some published views of their response to the Ulster Workers' Council (UWC) in 1974 and the 1985 Anglo-Irish Agreement. Bryett provides an examination of police decision making on a number of fronts and seeks to determine if we can learn anything new or different about policing in Northern Ireland.

Bryett states that despite the fragile solution to the 1995 Drumcree crisis, the significance of the problems in 1996 lie in the fact that they occurred in a period of relative calm. He discusses the events of Drumcree in 1996 and suggests that the problems for the RUC began when the Chief Constable decreed that the Orangemen would not be permitted to make their way along the Garvaghy Road. Due to sheer scale of numbers with 15,000 Orangemen confronting 3,000 police and soldiers, the Chief Constable was forced into an embarrassing about face and allowed the parade. The media witnessed police using batons against Garvaghy protestors, which suggested a heavy-handed response by a police intent on clearing the way for triumphant 'loyalists', even if this was not the case. Bryett suggests that this approach did little to alter the perception of many nationalist residents of the RUC as a partisan police force. He contends that in cordoning off loyalist roadblocks and allowing them to run their course, the police were protecting unlawful demonstrators from the public. Despite the police arguing that this was to prevent a breach of the peace, Bryett contends that this was not sound policing practice.

The section assesses the policing of comparable events in previous years and the precarious domestic position of the RUC during the 1985/1986 period of unrest, as over 500 officers were forced from their homes within loyalist areas following the Anglo-Irish Agreement. He compares this period with times of more favourable relations between the RUC and loyalists, such as those during the Ulster Workers' Council strike in 1974. He concludes that the UWC strike, the Anglo-Irish Agreement and Drumcree 1996 highlight that there may well be a point when, in the absence of strong organisational policy and government leadership, the stance to uphold law and order may be threatened by loyalties which are more deep-seated than institutional ones. This he argues is the result of the pressures of local tribalism since the RUC is a force that is overwhelmingly Protestant. He suggests that Northern Ireland's electorate must take substantial blame for Drumcree 1996, as the democratic principle gave way to adopting the most politically expedient way out of a very difficult problem. Due to the nature of upholding law and order in a state seen by many as illegitimate, policing becomes a major problem in organisational terms. Bryett believes that there has been slow progress, but bias still exists, and Drumcree 1996 did not help the cause of the RUC in terms of its public profile. This criticism he believes will continue until the political will emerges for more radical change.

13. **Buckley, Anthony D. and Kenney, Mary Catherine (1995)** *Negotiating Identity: Rhetoric, Metaphor and Social Drama in Northern Ireland.* **Washington, Smithsonian Institute Press.**

Chapter 10: *Fighting and Fun: Stone-Throwers and Spectators in Ulster Riots* discusses the links between riots and parades during the Protestant marching season in Northern Ireland. It focuses on particular riots linked to processions on Woodhouse Street, Obins Street, Falls Road and the Ardoyne. The chapter concludes that it is out of carnival-like loyalist and republican festivals that many riots actually develop, and suggests that the framework of a playful carnival is partly responsible for the frequency and pattern of rioting in Northern Ireland.

Chapter 11: *The Chosen Few: Biblical Texts in a Society with Secrets* focuses on the symbolism of the Royal Black Institution, which Buckley sees as a moderate and more religious society than other organisations. The chapter argues that the continuing popularity of the Royal Black Institution is due in part to the perceived relevance of their religious metaphors and texts to social, political and religious issues in Ulster. It is suggested that the biblical texts used by the Royal Black Institution provide a set of metaphors that allow them to see themselves in a similar respect to the Israelites, Jews and Christians in the Bible as God's chosen few. These biblical images reinforce the standard forms of Protestant rhetoric and it is claimed that of the three Loyal Order organisations the Royal Black Institution has the most extensive symbolism, which although constructed in secret is displayed regularly in parades and processions.

The chapter notes that biblical texts occur in four major contexts in the Black Institution, which include rituals, emblems, banners and sermons. Royal Black banners are discussed and the chapter notes the biblical pictures, which provide an interpretation of the biblical texts referred to. It is contended that any attempts to show what meanings these texts might have for an Ulster Protestant in the Black Preceptory are hindered by the fact that Orangemen and Blackmen are often unwilling to discuss matters with outsiders and that the initiation rites themselves are rarely discussed even amongst members.

Buckley examines the layers of meaning in the symbolism of the Black Institution, which include the emblem on the banner itself and the meaning to be found in the words of the texts. By identifying with the Israelites, the texts provide Blackmen with a means to explore a central feature of their fixed situation and relations between Catholics and Protestants. The chapter discusses a limited sample of banner pictures from annual Royal Black demonstrations in Antrim, Dromore and Lisburn on the last Saturday of August in 1982. Fourteen of the most characteristic texts are listed, with a number of references to the Israelites and the Old Testament, and there is a dominant pattern of an individual or group of people who have found favour in the eyes of God and who are also confronting an alien people, some of whom are wicked, some foreign and some of a rival religion. Another key theme is faithfulness and loyalty to God, and Buckley believes that the symbolism suggests that like the Israelites in Canaan, the Ulster Protestants have been given and occupy a foreign land. The section concludes that the symbolism of the Royal Black Institution reflects a tendency in Ulster Protestantism to conceive of themselves as a select group of people who have an especially close relationship to God. The emblems and images relate to a set of different stories which are in turn used as metaphors to define practical circumstances and the symbols have a direct bearing on the practical construction of an Ulster Protestant identity.

14. Cecil, Roseanne (1993) The Marching Season in Northern Ireland: An Expression of a Politico-Religious Identity. In MacDonald, Sharon (ed.) *Inside European Identities: Ethnography in Western Europe.* Oxford, Berg.

This chapter examines the concept of identity of the people of one small anonymised town in Northern Ireland, which Cecil calls 'Glengow', and discusses a number of aspects of politico-religious identity, with particular focus on the marching season. The author alleges that assumptions about the association between religious identity and political allegiance are widely held in Northern Ireland. Cecil describes the pattern of settlement in the town, which is described as a predominantly Protestant rural town located near to a republican area, and states that questions surrounding identity and the 'telling' of one's religion occurs partly through the explicit expression of identity which occurs on ritual occasions for both communities, mainly during the marching season. She describes politico-religious displays of the marching season, which are inextricably linked to political ideals and aspirations, and describes the scene in the town in the run up to the marching season. The author outlines that the lack of ritual in the Protestant churches of Northern Ireland is compensated for by the large number of Protestant men who are Orangemen and take part in rituals through the symbolism of the Orange Order. The chapter outlines two cases of sectarian display and ritual. The first focuses on a loyalist display and the build up to the Twelfth of July. Cecil sets out a chronology of events, describes the actions of the marching bands as deliberately provocative towards Catholics and mentions a heightened atmosphere of sectarianism around this time. The meaning and significance of the many symbols which are displayed by lodges on their banners and on Orange arches are said by Orangemen to be understood by all Orangemen and not by outsiders.

The second case of sectarian display involves a Lady's Day parade by the Ancient Order of Hibernians on 15 August. Cecil documents the role of the Royal Ulster Constabulary towards the march, and argues that while there are similarities between the style of the AOH event and the Twelfth, the events highlighted the fundamental differences between the two occasions and the two groups of participants. For Protestants, the Twelfth is a celebration of an event that took place many years before and asserted both their historical and contemporary dominance over Catholics, with the police seen as 'their' police. The AOH event is not seen as a celebration, rather as rebellion and an act of defiance and anger against the state and what is perceived to not be 'their' police. Cecil claims that the meanings of the two events are totally different, with the Twelfth event asserting dominance and the AOH event being one of rebellion. Protestants are said to place the greater claim upon Glengow by marching through its streets as part of their annual celebration in a way that Catholics cannot do. The chapter concludes that in Glengow generally, politico-religious differences are not discussed, but the explicit public expression of politico-religious identity is sanctioned on specific ritual occasions.

15. **Committee on the Administration of Justice (1996)** *The Misrule of Law: A Report on the Policing of Events During the Summer of 1996 in Northern Ireland.* **Belfast, Committee on the Administration of Justice.**

The document draws upon detailed reports from a team of international observers at twenty contentious parades and demonstrations between late

June and early September of 1996. In addition to this, the authors took statements from individuals with first hand accounts of the events in 1996. The Committee on the Administration of Justice (CAJ) suggest that there needs to be an international and independent inquiry to ascertain any justification for certain operational decisions. The publication argues that the law in Northern Ireland has consistently failed to guarantee equal and adequate protection for the rights and liberties of every person. CAJ contend that the violence associated with the summer of 1996 is not just the result of inter-communal conflict and that it is the responsibility of the civil and legal authorities in Northern Ireland to maintain a framework of the rule of law which protects the rights of all. The report highlights the issue of public order for the police, and suggests that there should be a balance between different needs and rights, outlining that there are no over-arching rights on either side.

The report notes what it believes may be the possible sectarian use of plastic bullets, and reports RUC statistics which highlight that only 662 plastic bullets were discharged against unionists, while 5,340 were discharged against nationalists during disturbances. The authors also suggest that plastic bullets were fired from too close a distance and often at the upper body of individuals, both against regulations. In Derry Londonderry on 11 and 13 July, CAJ conclude that the actions taken by the security forces were not always in response to a dangerous incident, but frequently contributed to the creation of such a situation, and are critical that police and army procedure/guidance for the use of plastic bullets is not in the public domain. The report is critical of police tactics and accuses the RUC of moving obstructions, hemming people in, engaging in poor communication with protestors, using Land Rovers aggressively, and adopting an overall aggressive policing style coupled with an ill-chosen selection of weaponry. CAJ criticise the Chief Constable's reversal of his decision over the parade at Drumcree, which they suggest for many merely confirms their belief that the RUC is a partisan police force.

The booklet discusses in more detail several more serious specific incidents which occurred, including the death of Dermot McShane who was crushed by an army Saracen, an alleged baton charge in Altnagelvin hospital by the RUC and a near curfew on the Lower Ormeau Road on the Twelfth. The authors claim that there are two contradictory rights at issue: the right of the marchers to parade without fear of attack and the right of residents to freedom of movement. They believe that there was unequal treatment in relation to Drumcree and the Ormeau Road, with unionist crowds allowed to gather at Drumcree while Lower Ormeau was virtually swamped with security forces.

The document moves on to highlight international and domestic legal perspectives, and the chapter specifically addresses public order, police accountability, the use of force, marching and human rights and government responses. CAJ contend that it is not appropriate for the police to wait until the last minute to determine who appears likely to cause most disruption, and they also condemn the police ability to be able to take both the decision in relation to routing/re-routing and enforcing the decisions once taken. The report also suggests that a completely independent police complaints system is needed.

The report assesses the International Covenant on Civil and Political Rights and the European Convention of Human Rights, while noting that the Organisation for Security and Cooperation in Europe makes it clear that minorities cannot be subjected to any form of discrimination. A key argument the report forwards is that both marchers and residents' groups in Northern Ireland have sustainable arguments in International Law to support their respective positions, and marchers can cite the ICCPR and ECHR while residents can assert their rights to parity of esteem, non-discrimination and their right to freedom of movement under OSCE provisions. There needs to be a balance, with the right to march being understood as deriving from International Human Rights Law, but is not absolute and the government is equally obligated to protect minority rights. It is noted that there is little outlined in international law which lays down the principle of consent.

The report recommends the establishment of a Commission on Policing to look into the future of policing while investigating the events of the summer, and calls for an immediate end to the use of plastic bullets alongside a review of the use of the weapon. CAJ also call for a public and independent inquiry into the death of Dermot McShane to establish the facts of the case, and suggest that the findings of an internal inquiry into the incident at Altnagelvin hospital should be made public. The report suggests a need for new provisions to better balance conflicting rights and provide effective remedies for appeal, while making the Secretary of State's powers reviewable by the courts. CAJ call for an independent system of dealing with complaints of the police. In terms of marching and human rights, the report concludes that there are no absolute rights and the principle of proportionality is key, and also that decisions about marching must reflect the key principle that everyone is equal before the law.

16. **Committee on the Administration of Justice (1997)** *Policing the Police: A Report on the Policing of Events During the Summer of 1997 in Northern Ireland.* **Belfast, Committee on the Administration of Justice.**

This report begins by briefly summarising the CAJ 1996 report 'The Misrule of Law' and compares the situation in 1997 with that of a year previously, concluding that in 1997 there were fewer examples of protestors being physically moved by the police. It suggests that according to observers, police tactics involving the use of batons were overly aggressive. The report is partly based on witness statements taken from the Garvaghy Road in July 1997. CAJ critique the close physical contact between the police and demonstrators when firearms are involved and suggest that communication skills were lacking at important moments. These included inadequate warnings about police intentions prior to rapid deployment, which led to misleading or incorrect information. This is claimed to have only exacerbated tensions between marchers and residents. CAJ believe that communication in 1997 was worse than it had been previously, although they cite the situation in Pomeroy as an example of better practice and communication.

They outline difficulties with police Land Rovers, such as the lack of an easily identifiable licence plate, and they also suggest that the wearing of riot gear by police can inflame tensions. The report is critical of the fact that the police did not use new powers to control the public consumption of alcohol, and notes the fact that twice the annual average number of plastic bullets were fired in just three nights in Derry Londonderry as for the whole of the period between 1982 and 1995.

The publication highlights the difficulty of the police and army operating under different legislation than elsewhere, and suggests that a number of plastic bullets fired in 1996 were defective. Other problems associated with plastic bullets were the lack of a warning given prior to firing, the problems associated with ricocheting bullets and the intimidatory nature of the weapons. The authors suggest that it is key that police officers have some form of ID clearly visible, otherwise there is a lack of police accountability for officers' actions on the ground. The report is critical of the Chief Constable and the lack of statistics on plastic bullets, highlighting weak RUC record keeping and accountability mechanisms as unsatisfactory, while also outlining some new problems in 1997 not present in 1996. These include the decision making process, which the report argues should be based on international principles of human rights and not on threats of violence. Secondly, the authors criticise the army's role in policing, and thirdly the report is critical of the police and army's use of video cameras.

CAJ state that they believe the marching issue will only be resolved if the rights of both marchers and residents are accorded equal respect and enshrined in international human rights principles, and when there is a balance of rights, which seeks to look beyond public order considerations. The authors recommend that where possible there should be a reliance on local accommodations to achieve a settlement. The document concludes with some proposed actions for the public, which include writing to the Secretary of State, Chief Constable and Chair of the Police Authority. The publication also contains a supplement entitled 'Policing the Police: The Video' which is based on a video produced on the policing of contentious events during the 1995/1996/1997 marching seasons.

17. de Rosa, Ciro (1998) Playing Nationalism. In Buckley, Anthony D. (ed.) *Symbols in Northern Ireland*. Belfast, Institute of Irish Studies.

This chapter is based on interviews with several members of four Belfast based flute bands and is concerned with parades and demonstrations among nationalists in Northern Ireland. It aims to show how nationalist symbols provide an important cultural resource for working class Catholic youths who are members of republican flute and drum bands. De Rosa defines ritual and highlights its key relationship with symbolism and states that rituals represent symbolic devices, which keep people aware of their sense of belonging to a community and define 'us' and 'them'. He analyses how rituals produce the symbolisation of community boundaries and investigates the competing discourses and negotiation of meaning, which take place during ceremonies.

It is argued that both communities in Northern Ireland share a fundamental symbolism, although nationalist bands do not seem to play the fundamental role that the loyalist bands play on the Twelfth. De Rosa discusses the Ancient Order of Hibernians and their marching tradition, describing the organisation and structure, and outlines differences between the Feast of Assumption and the Twelfth of July. Firstly, the AOH have not held the same political and economic power as Orangemen; secondly, the AOH have not been as predominant in the nationalist community as the Orange Order have in the unionist community and thirdly the Twelfth is a public festival while the Feast of Assumption is not.

The musical bands of these parading organisations provide an important means whereby young people can become engaged in political activity. The phenomenon of republican bands is a relatively new one by Northern Ireland standards and really developed after the hunger strikes in 1981. The band is said to symbolise group identity whether it be of family or of Irish heritage and it plays an important social role in local communities. De Rosa identifies locality as more important to loyalists than to republican bands and concludes that nationalist and republican ideology and its symbols provide the marginalized working class with symbols of success and social promotion placed beyond the rhythms of working life. The bands develop what de Rosa terms a 'Provo' sub-culture using the symbolism of rebellion and opposition by violent means if necessary.

18. **Dickson, Bruce and Hamilton, Michael (2003) Meetings and Marches. In Dickson, Bruce and O'Brien, Martin (eds.) *Civil Liberties in Northern Ireland: Fourth Edition*. Belfast, Committee on the Administration of Justice.**

Chapter Eight *Marches and Meetings* documents the legislation dealing with marches and meetings in Northern Ireland specifically and the UK more generally and contends that, prior to the 1998 Human Rights Act, the right to public assembly was not explicitly guaranteed by law. The European Court has held that there have been unnecessary violations of the right to peaceful assembly on two occasions and the court has outlined some general principles regarding the interpretation of Article 11 of the European Convention of Human Rights. These include: that those who wish to exercise the right of peaceful assembly must have peaceful intentions, that restrictions should not be based on perceptions of others and may legitimately cause offence and that the right to counter demonstrate should not be allowed to inhibit the right to demonstrate.

Dickson and Hamilton note that it is still unclear when exactly a march can be stopped or rerouted under Article 11 (2) of the ECHR. The chapter outlines that in the UK the courts have not generally distinguished between sources of disorder, even if that disorder emanates from opponents of a procession. It has been argued that if antagonism will considerably increase disruptions to the life of the community, rerouting may be justified. In Northern Ireland, the power to impose conditions is held under Article 4 (2) of the 1987 Public Order (Northern Ireland) Order, whereby a senior police officer may impose conditions if he/she believes the assembly will create serious disorder, damage property, cause serious disruption to commercial life or intimidate others.

The authors highlight that only the Secretary of State can ban open air public meetings under Article 5 of the 1987 Public Order (Northern Ireland) Order which was amended in the 1998 Act, if there is a threat of serious public disorder, a serious disruption to community life and if the parade will cause undue demands on the police and the military. It is further suggested that where a parade passes through a residential area or an area of high commercial activity, the organisation in question should give local people as much prior notice as possible. This could perhaps entail advertisements in local newspapers, flyers or posters and should specify the date and time of the parade, the route, numbers taking part, the number of bands, arrangements for its control and the name and address of the organiser.

It is documented that the Public Processions (Northern Ireland) Act of 1998 extended the statutory criteria for determining if conditions should be imposed, moving away from decisions based solely on public order grounds. Section 8 (6) of the Act outlines that the Parades Commission must have regard to any possible public disorder or damage to property, any disruption to the life of the community, the impact on relationships within the community, any failure to comply with the code of conduct and the desirability of allowing a parade along a customarily held route.

The authors conclude that Northern Ireland has unique provision for the control of bands, with Section 12 of the 1998 Act allowing the Secretary of State to require bands to be registered and anyone knowingly parading with an unregistered band can face six months imprisonment and a fine of up to five thousand pounds. It is an offence under Article 18 of the 1987 Act for a person to use riotous behaviour that is likely to disturb the peace and a 1992 decision in the Northern Ireland Court of Appeal ruled that words alone could constitute disorderly behaviour. Despite concerns at levels of disorder at some parades in Northern Ireland, the report outlines that PSNI statistics show that in 2001-2002 there was disorder at only twenty eight of 2,808 parades, most of which involved obstruction by people sitting in public places in protest.

19. **Dunn, Seamus (2000) Bloody Sunday and its Commemorative Parades. In, Fraser, T.G. (ed.)** *The Irish Parading Tradition: Following the Drum.* **Basingstoke, Macmillan.**

This chapter focuses on the events of Bloody Sunday in Derry Londonderry in 1969 and outlines that when those who represent the state disturb public order with violence and death, especially in Ireland with the contested nature of the northern state, the events have a symbolic and emotional significance and have a transformative impact on public imagination. Dunn outlines that there has been a march to commemorate Bloody Sunday every year since the event and the chapter argues that the march has evolved over the years, reflecting a number of other processes at work. These processes include the changing relationships between the Social Democratic and Labour Party (SDLP) and Sinn Féin, and the Official and Provisional IRA among others. The author discusses the context of Bloody Sunday and notes that the first anniversary commemoration in 1973 attracted a crowd of 15,000, with the pattern of two events repeated each year since, a non-political small wreath laying ceremony and Sinn Féin's annual march.

Dunn claims that there are essentially two marches: the Northern Ireland Civil Rights Association and Official IRA march attracting about 2,000 people and the Sinn Féin march attracting 5,000 people. The year 1976 saw tensions developing between different groups, and the author believes that there was a channelling and exploitation of the Bloody Sunday experience, and that since Internment in 1975 and the 1981 hunger strikes, the IRA have become more acceptable to many people otherwise opposed to violence. The essay discusses the formation in 1986 of the Bloody Sunday Organising Committee, which with Sinn Féin speakers criticised the position of the SDLP. Despite this, the 1988 Hume/Adams dialogue helped create changes in approach by the parties to Bloody Sunday and from April 1992 a new group, the Bloody Sunday Justice Campaign, was formed. These new and relatively harmonious relations were highlighted by the parades of 1997 and 1998, which were the largest and most peaceful to date, and Dunn contends that these links have been further boosted by the launch of the Saville Enquiry in 1998.

20. **Dudley-Edwards, Ruth** (1999) *The Faithful Tribe: An Intimate Portrait of the Loyal Institutions.* **London, Harper Collins Publishers.**

This book takes an in depth look at the Loyal Institutions, with Dudley-Edwards feeling a certain empathy for the Orangemen in Northern Ireland, believing that bands and parades are part of the outward and visible culture of the majority of the Ulster Protestant people. The book pays particular attention to the Drumcree crises of the mid to late 1990s. The author notes how her views towards the Orders changed over the years, her belief that the Orange Order in Northern Ireland is a Protestant means of male bonding and that their parades are a means of showing that they will not go away. Dudley-Edwards disputes the belief that Orange parades are essentially territorial and triumphalist, and cites the example of the Rossnowlagh parade in County Donegal in the Irish Republic as an example of what Orange parades are really about. Despite this, she accuses Orangemen of often shooting themselves in the foot, such as was the case in 1997 in Lurgan when the local Order hired a local 'Blood and Thunder' band which could invariably lead to outsiders leaving with an image of the Order as drum beating bigots.

The book outlines a number of reasons as to why individuals may join the Loyal Orders, including possible family connections, the role of the bands in the community, respect for others and a sense of history and religious tolerance. The author also describes how members join and outlines the qualifications of an Orangeman. Dudley-Edwards provides descriptions of differing viewpoints of the Twelfth and discusses the Loyal Order's regalia, banners and music, highlighting that many Orangemen see the 'Blood and Thunder' bands as a safety valve for young men in stopping them joining loyalist paramilitary organisations.

Dudley-Edwards argues that the presence of Mohawk Orange lodges and lodges in Togo and elsewhere in Africa suggests that, although the Order is routinely described as bigoted and fascist, it is in fact both international and non-racist. The differing role of women in the Orange Order is noted, as in West Africa, New Zealand and Australia many lodges are mixed in gender. In Northern Ireland, women must be invited to take part in a parade and have their own separate Order. There are also differences in the ceremonies, rituals and degrees in the different jurisdictions.

The author discusses the background to the increasing religious divisions, which led to the formation of the Order, arguing that the main founders of the Orange Order were the Irish Volunteers, and parades and processions provided the flashpoint between Protestant agrarian societies such as the Peep O'Day boys and the Catholic Defenders. She sees the setting up of a respectable umbrella organisation as an attempt to take a stand in defence of the crown and Protestant religion, and discusses the attractions of joining Orange societies. Firstly, they offer mutual protection against known and unknown enemies; secondly, they provide the mysteries of freemasonry and thirdly, their parades and ceremonies emulate the Volunteers. Dudley-Edwards contends that from the beginning Orange secrets were based on the biblical saga of the exodus of the children of Israel. The growth of Orangeism was seen as inevitable and in the north particularly landlords encouraged their tenants to join Orangeism both as a defensive organisation and as a way of constraining 'hot heads'.

It is noted that the reputation of the Orange Order at Dolly's Brae in 1849 was at its lowest point ever and that the leadership accepted the Party Processions Act of 1850, although the rank and file were not prepared to accept any ban on parades, especially in areas such as Sandy Row. This period saw very serious sectarian riots in Belfast in 1857, 1864, 1872 and

1886. The Order is seen as a vital instrument in bringing the new working class votes into new divisional associations and the book examines the background to home rule in the late nineteenth century, a period when there was much loyalist violence, which often centred around parades. The author suggests that by this period Orange parades were enriched by accordion, flute, pipe and silver bands and that the development of the railways made massive demonstrations possible. This era also saw the development of Ulster Unionism, which relied heavily on the Orange Order for support.

The formation of the state of Northern Ireland as what is described as an 'Orange State' led to unionist leaders keeping their electorate in the fold by wearing Orange collarettes and making defiant speeches on the Twelfth. During this period, Orange parades still provided flashpoints at times of sectarian tension, but Dudley-Edwards asserts that the vast majority were peaceful and enjoyed by members of both traditions. Dudley-Edwards cites accounts of Orangemen in rural areas as having close relationships and co-operation with Catholics. She argues that by the early 1970s, the Provisional IRA were using Orange marches as a pretext for trying to destabilise the state of Northern Ireland and that this led to the strategy leading to the Drumcree dispute of 1995.

The book also charts the rise of the nationalist residents' groups, which developed at a time when there was an attack on the more moderate leadership of the Orange Order from within, led by Joel Patton and the Spirit of Drumcree group. Dudley-Edwards argues that a decision was taken to step up normal levels of opposition to parades by the Loyal Orders and to make them the focus for republican discontent. The role of Gerard Rice, Donncha MacNiallais and Breandan MacCionnaith is assessed and the book claims that they were chosen as community representatives deliberately as they had convictions for terrorist offences and therefore the Loyal Orders would almost certainly refuse to engage with them.

The first Drumcree dispute in 1995 is described in some detail and it is contended that the fundamental message that this event sent to both loyalist and republican paramilitaries was that decisions were taken based on which side could cause the most public disorder. By the time of the second dispute at Drumcree in 1996, the parades issue was becoming a disaster for the Orange Order, as the 1995 events at Drumcree had polarized the two communities and led to more militant elements joining the dispute. This also led to a split in the Order between more moderate and hard-line elements. The violence of 1996 saw Orangemen rise to the status of an international pariah, although Dudley-Edwards believes that most

Orangemen stayed peaceful and tried to maintain discipline. The author notes that at this point she was concerned at what appeared to be a drift in 1996 in the Orange leadership's focus and direction.

She highlights the negative role that can be played by more rowdy 'Blood and Thunder' bands and that this in turn affected efforts at mediation in Dromore and elsewhere. The tensions inherent within the Order during this period between moderates such as William Bingham and hard-liners who scuppered attempts at deals with residents are examined. This continuing battle between the Orange moderates and extremists took place against the backdrop of talks on a constitutional settlement and the Good Friday Agreement hardened attitudes among Orangemen further. Dudley-Edwards is critical of the extremist leadership of both the Garvaghy Residents and the Spirit of Drumcree group.

The book concludes with a critical view of the Parades Commission and states that it was a disaster waiting to happen, took no account of the importance of local issues and local territory, and the British government should have paid more attention to the Loyal Orders and less to the Dublin government. The publication concludes that the Drumcree situation only seemed to reward intransigence, and that the dithering of the Orange leadership and signing of the Good Friday Agreement in 1998 led to the whole Orange Order becoming split over the strategy and tactics that should be adopted to try and resolve the situation.

21. Farrell, Sean (2000) *Rituals and Riots: Sectarian Violence and Political Culture in Ulster 1784-1886.* **Lexington, University Press Kentucky.**

The book examines the process and nature of sectarian violence in late eighteenth and nineteenth century Ulster and analyses the relationship between sectarian riots and the evolution of the North's divided political culture, linking sectarian riots to issues related to power and control. The study begins by highlighting the impact of Dolly's Brae on the Twelfth in 1849 as a major sectarian flashpoint of the nineteenth century. Farrell documents the importance of the role of Catholic women at the forefront of the opposition to the Orange Order parade at Dolly's Brae, which resulted in thirty Catholics being killed and the introduction of the new Party Processions Act of 1850.

Chapter One *Trouble in Armagh, 1784-1798* charts the development of conflict between the Protestant Peep O'Day Boys and the Catholic Defenders dating from 1784. The author suggests that these troubles in

Armagh began because mid-Ulster loyalists perceived powerful forces working to overwhelm the sectarian moral economy, which was an exclusivist definition of loyalty and citizenship. At the heart of this sectarian moral economy was a special relationship between the Protestant gentry and plebeian Protestants, and the rise of the Irish Volunteers and threat to this order led to the Protestant elites taking steps to revitalize their ties to the lower-classes. The chapter provides a detailed examination of the Battle of the Diamond in September 1795, which according to Farrell led to two key developments: the formation of the Orange Order and the Armagh expulsions of 1795-1796.

Chapter Two *The Orange Order and Catholic Resistance 1795-1820* cites the 1813 riot in Belfast as the first organized sectarian riot between Orange and Green in the nineteenth century. The formation of the Orange Order and Ribbon societies greatly enhanced the structured nature of party violence. Farrell claims that almost any sectarian riot of pre-famine Ulster was directly tied to provocative actions of the Orange Order or their Catholic enemies. This chapter examines the critical role played by partisan institutions in sectarian violence of the early nineteenth century and focuses on the relationships between these evolving partisan institutions, popular politics and sectarian contention. The chapter also examines the formation of the Orange Order and argues that two factors set the Order apart from its predecessors, the ability to act as an umbrella organisation and the ability to attract elite Protestant support.

The chapter also documents Ulster Catholic resistance from 1800-1820, charts the evolution of underground Catholic political organisations between 1798 and 1848 and views Catholic participation in early nineteenth century sectarian conflict as a communal response to the Orange Order's partisan dominance. Farrell documents the critical role of Catholic women in most attempts to block Orange marches and asserts that riots represented one of the few public spaces where female participation was not only tolerated, but welcomed. Farrell contends that, like Defenderism, Ulster Ribbonism was a product of an Orange attempt to re-impose its exclusivist vision of the sectarian moral economy onto Ulster society. The chapter concludes by contrasting the decline of the Orange Order between 1815 and 1821 due to the lack of a real threat, with the rise in the Catholic marching 'tradition'.

Chapter Three *National Politics and Sectarian Violence 1821-1829* suggests that the 1880s was the low point of the Orange Order's existence to date, although with the re-emergence of a serious Catholic threat, Orangemen responded by using ritualised displays of strength and violence to reaffirm their ascendant position. Farrell notes that there were twice as many sectarian riots in 1826-1829 compared to 1821-1825.

Chapter Four *Ritual and Sectarian Violence* links public rituals and communal violence, with an estimated six of the fifteen largest riots in nineteenth century Belfast stemming directly from Orange processions. This chapter discusses the motivations of rioters themselves, the lower-class Catholics and Protestants. Farrell outlines the messages he believes are contained within Orange parades, within which he includes those of power and ascendancy, territorial control and a desire to legitimise the ideology of the Order and strengthen its self-image as the champion of Protestantism.

Chapter Five *Urbanization and Sectarian Rioting in mid-Victorian Ulster* analyses aspects of the urbanization process that created an environment ripe for sectarian violence and argues that after 1843 and the rioting in Belfast, sectarian violence in Ulster by the middle of the century had become a largely urban phenomenon due to industrialization. Farrell is critical of Boyd and Baker's 'Two Phase' approach of conflict in nineteenth century Belfast and argues that the underlying factor was that there were two conflicting visions of how Irish society should be structured. He asserts that Belfast provided an almost perfect environment for ritualised sectarian conflict that characterized the nineteenth century, as provocative incidents could easily be manufactured, and it is no coincidence that the 'age of riots' coincided with the forces of industrialization, urbanization and democratisation. The author claims that the segregated environment, which led to the development of areas like the Pound and Sandy Row, was a near perfect arena for party processions. These ritual invasions went hand in hand with riots such as those in 1857, 1864 and 1872. The chapter discusses the riots between the Pound and Sandy Row between 1832 and 1869, and also describes two Belfast riots in 1843 and in 1857 and one in Derry Londonderry in 1869 in detail. It appears that several factors converged in the late 1860s to accelerate the pace of sectarian confrontation, the re-emergence of Irish revolutionary nationalism, William Johnston's campaign against the Party Processions Act and Gladstone's disestablishment of the Church of Ireland, all of which contributed to loyalist insecurity and led to violence.

Chapter Six *The Campaign to Repeal the Party Processions Act: 1860-1872* discusses William Johnston's populist campaign to repeal the Party

Processions Act. Johnston's successful campaign to regain the Orangemen's right to walk played a critical role in reanimating the system of cross-class Protestant collaboration that would later provide the essential foundation for Ulster unionism. The author notes that the role of the Orange elite and the Anglican clergy lent credibility to Johnston's campaign and more people became involved in public demonstrations. This had a direct impact on communal relations and between 1868-1872 there was an increase in the level of sectarian conflict, with a surge in loyalist marching from 1868.

The second part of chapter six, *Sectarian Violence and the formation of Modern Ulster Politics* notes that by the mid-1880s the political middle ground had disappeared and the election of 1885, coupled with the first Home Rule bill in 1886, led to the Orange Order having a disproportionate influence at this time. The subsequent ties between the Order and Ulster Unionism lent credibility to the Order and Orangeism began to move to the centre of Ulster Protestantism in 1886. The book concludes that by continually replaying the traumatic events of the seventeenth century, and most notably the events of 1690 at the Boyne, processions and the violence produced maintained the relevance of a political discourse centred on sectarian division. Farrell believes that virtually every communal riot originated in a perceived threat to an Irish polity structured upon Protestant privilege.

22. Fraser, T. G. (2000) The Apprentice Boys and Relief of Derry Parades. In Fraser, T.G. (ed.) *The Irish Parading Tradition: Following the Drum.* Basingstoke, Macmillan.

This section explores the history of the traditions of marching to celebrate the siege of Derry and notes the role of Colonel John Mitchelburne in keeping them alive. The author believes that the first possible club of the Apprentice Boys could have been as early as 1714 and documents that early celebrations of the siege even involved the Catholic bishop in 1788 and 1789. By 1798 the political climate had changed, mainly in response to increasing Catholic migration into Derry Londonderry, and after the formation of the first Apprentice Boys of Derry Club in 1814 there was turbulence over the next few years. The author states that the celebrations were banned in 1832 for five years. According to Fraser, it was not until the reconstitution of the Apprentice Boys of Derry in 1835 that the modern organisation really began.

The author claims that unionist self-confidence in the 1960s was reflected in Apprentice Boys' parades and the chapter describes the situation at the

1969 parade when two things agitated residents, the throwing of coins and loyalist women singing 'The Sash'. This relief parade had provided the catalyst and changed forever the political face of Northern Ireland and the collapse of unionist power in the city led to the Apprentice Boys struggling to keep their relief celebrations alive. There was a dramatic expansion of the Apprentice Boys' clubs from the 1970s onwards, as this was a time when Protestants felt under siege from both the IRA and the government, and 1975 saw the first west bank parade in Derry Londonderry since 1969. It is argued that this parade took place because two main areas of tension were gone, the demographic changes meaning that there was no city-side route available and secondly that for security purposes the walls of the city were now closed. The chapter states that in general there has been an overall easing of the parading situation in the city and in 1994 the Apprentice Boys paraded a section of the walls for the first time since 1969.

Despite this, Fraser outlines two reasons why 1995 was such a contentious parade. He contends that this resulted from the walls being open after the ceasefires, which meant that any parade would necessarily pass the Bogside. He also suggests that the situation at Drumcree in July of the same year had raised passions. The chapter proceeds to describe the build up in tension prior to the proposed parade and states that the lack of a police decision by 12 August increased the tension further. It documents the principle of consent as espoused by the Bogside Residents Group, Lower Ormeau Concerned Community and the Garvaghy Road Residents' Coalition. The march finally took place on 19 October, with the Apprentice Boys resting their case on the right to celebrate an event at the heart of their history and culture, and the important symbolism of the walls, war memorial and cathedral. They saw their right to parade as the test of the continuing acceptability of the minority Protestant population in the city, and the question of how the relief parades were to be held was a touchstone for how the two communities regarded each other's rights and heritage.

23. **Fraser, Grace and Morgan, Valerie (2000) Miracle on the Shankill: The Peace March and Rally of 28th August 1976. In Fraser, T.G. (ed.)** *The Irish Parading Tradition: Following the Drum.* **Basingstoke, Macmillan.**

This section discusses the background to the formation of the Peace People, established by Mairead Corrigan, Betty Williams and Ciaran McKeown, who organised a peace march on the Shankill Road on 28 August 1976 and which significantly involved both Catholics and Protestants. The numbers involved in the march were estimated to be between 20,000-25,000.

The chapter discusses the organisation of the event itself and highlights that the Peace People themselves regarded the marching element as indispensable to the success and impact of the day. Up until the formation of the movement, individuals had been gathering spontaneously with little effect, but this parade brought people together in huge numbers, despite the authors noting that the march organisers were worried about the paramilitary response. Fraser and Morgan claim that the interaction of a number of factors determined what happened and that the organisation of large-scale rallies could not be sustained over a prolonged period. They suggest that this is why within a year support for the movement was difficult to secure despite mass antipathy to violence.

The chapter asserts that an analysis of a public march through the territory of the 'other' community seems particularly relevant in the context of the emergence of contentious parades as one of the major issues of the late 1990s. The authors outline why the Shankill March did not turn into a Drumcree type situation. They argue that the symbolism of women and peace is important, and given the history of symbolism of women in Ireland it makes it difficult to openly attack women. The chapter concludes that one key problem facing the movement was that it had a licence to break the rules in the short-term, but could be marginalized in the longer-term by the traditional power blocs.

24. Garvaghy Residents (1999) *Garvaghy: A Community Under Siege.* Belfast, Beyond the Pale Publications.

This publication contains a series of contributions in the form of brief personal diaries from residents of the Garvaghy Road focusing on the events of July 1998. The book suggests that its main purpose is to provide contemporary accounts in words and pictures of what it is like to live in the Garvaghy area during the 'marching season'. The diaries document difficulties they feel they have during the marching season, with a particular focus on the lack of access to the town centre, a feeling of being 'hemmed in' in one's own community and the negative role of tranquillisers, medication and other sedatives. They also talk about the effects on their children who did not understand what was going on. Some respondents also felt some guilt over the deaths of the three Quinn children in 1998, who were killed by a loyalist petrol bomb after the Drumcree parade was stopped.

The publication also contains an edited and updated version of a submission made by the Garvaghy Road Residents' Coalition to the

Independent Review of Parades and Marches in November 1996, which was critical of police restrictions on nationalist parades. It also forwards residents' views on parades in a divided society, and the residents argue that Orange parades are about flaunting the symbols of Protestant supremacy and the culture of unionist domination.

The book provides a history of previous violent clashes in Portadown between 1795 and 1912, and the July 1969, 1972 and 1983 disturbances in Obins street. The residents argue that it was during the 1981 H-Block protests that the first real attempt to develop an organised response to Orange parades occurred. The role of the Drumcree Faith and Justice Group between 1988 and 1994 is examined, with the 1995 parade crisis leading to the formation of the Garvaghy Road Residents' Group. There is a detailed description of the events of 1995 from the perspective of the residents of the road.

The publication concludes with a proposal to the Orange Order of two alternative routes to march, either from the town centre via Corcrain Road, Charles Street and the Dungannon Road returning by the same route, or alternatively from the town centre via Loughgall Road, Corcillentragh and across to Drumcree Road again returning the same way.

25. Hadden, Tom and Donnelly, Anne (1997) *The Legal Control of Marches in Northern Ireland.* Belfast, Community Relations Council.

This study analyses the law and the way in which it is enforced, and sets out some of the options for a possible change of criteria to permit or ban marches. The authors urge that any changes should be based on the principles of mutual respect and toleration in order to help promote a wider and longer lasting settlement in Northern Ireland.

Chapter One: *Introduction* begins by highlighting the difficulty of achieving political compromise during the marching season from Easter to August. The chapter discusses what it claims to be a clash of rights between those who assert their right to march on 'traditional' routes and those who insist on refusal in 'their own areas'. The report assesses the difficult questions that these differences pose for policy makers, with particular regard to the police role in controlling public order. The chapter suggests that parades should not simply be allowed due to a threat of violence and public disorder.

Chapter Two: *The Marching Traditions* highlights the imbalance in approach between Orange and Green marches, noting that republican parades have traditionally been banned from town and city centres, but most Orange marches were exempted from a requirement of prior notification given that they were 'customarily held over a particular route'. The chapter cites Royal Ulster Constabulary figures from 1985-1995 as signifying a huge imbalance between the number of loyalist and republican marches, with an estimated ten times as many loyalist marches taking place during this period. The chapter also highlights that objections to parades up to 1997 have led to five judicial reviews, mostly based on either traffic congestion or band members' behaviour.

Chapter Three: *The Legal Framework* suggests that until recently the power of the police to intervene to preserve public order was based on the concepts of breach of the peace and unlawful assembly. The chapter discusses common law and public order acts and cites several examples of court decisions and appeals against convictions of breach of the peace. The underlying principle is that the police may take whatever action they see fit to prevent a breach of the peace, regardless of the source of the threat, and common law has in this sense been superseded by the public order legislation. Hadden and Donnelly discuss the origins of these acts in the years of the Stormont regime, with particular reference to the regime's banning of a number of civil rights marches in 1968-1969. There was an implicit exemption in this legislation to established parades of the Loyal Orders. The chapter then proceeds to outline the rules set out by the 1987 Public Order (Northern Ireland) Order, and concludes that there was little prospect of the courts overruling a police decision and that there was effectively a statutory ban on any judicial review of decisions by or on behalf of the Secretary of State.

Chapter Four: *Assessment of the Current Regime* outlines that since 1980 there have been a number of significant changes in the legal regime governing parades. This period saw the elimination of the 'traditional procession' protection usually accorded to most Orange parades and saw the power of the police increased. Despite the new provisions, the chapter argues that the RUC gave primary consideration to the risk of public disorder and less weight to the new provisions to intervene on grounds of disruption to the local community or intimidation by those involved in a march. Hadden and Donnelly claim the problem lies with the way the current law is being implemented by the police and successive secretaries of state. The authors argue for the implementation of a comprehensive new regime to govern marches and demonstrations, which would have greater clarity and would command greater public support.

Chapter Five: *International Comparisons* gives a brief account of approaches in other jurisdictions and also provides an international legal overview of the situation.

Chapter Six: *International Human Rights Requirements* discusses those conventions which are binding on the UK as being the European Convention of Human Rights (Article 11) and the International Covenant on Civil and Political Rights (Article 21). These allow for the imposition of restrictions in the need for national security and public order. In terms of being relevant to Northern Ireland, the chapter mentions Article 27 of the International Covenant on Civil and Political Rights and the Copenhagen Document of the Organisation for Security and Co-operation in Europe (OSCE), which states that both communities have the right to enjoy their culture as well as to practise their religion and use their language, although the authors claim that even legal frameworks such as these give a lot of discretion to governments with regards to their implementation. The chapter suggests that the key element is proportionality. It concludes with a summary of the basic requirements for any new decisions deduced from the cases, that they should: take into account the rights and interests of both marchers and residents; give greater weight to the claims of those who are committed to peaceful protest than those who use or threaten violence; avoid discrimination and allow for an effective appeal by review.

Chapter Seven: *The Policy Options* suggests that if the marching problem could be solved it could point a way to a more general political settlement. Hadden and Donnelly state that there are three general policy approaches to marching which they assert are not mutually exclusive, the right to march, communal consent and communal accommodation.

Chapter Eight: *A New Public Order Order* claims that significant changes are needed to the Public Order (Northern Ireland) Order. There needs to be greater weight given to either a right to march, communal consent or a code of conduct. The chapter highlights two problems with intervention, that the police have not always used it constructively and that it was not possible to deal with more than one parade at a time. Hadden and Donnelly suggest that possible changes to the Order could involve authorised conditions such as restrictions on marchers' behaviour, conditions could be imposed as to the number of dates of marches in an area in a stated period, and that organisers should be required to give advance notification of all parades along a given route and longer than the current provision of seven days. The report states that there should be an independent element of some kind in the decision making process, and outlines four possibilities which include an increased role for the Secretary of State, an increased role for the courts, an independent tribunal and an increased role for mediation. The authors contend that sanctions should be imposed on those who do not comply with a code of conduct or the rulings of a tribunal.

Chapter Nine: *A Vision for the Future* provides a draft code of conduct and some proposed changes in the law. These include: a statutory code of conduct; initial decisions are to remain with the police; appeals to go to an independent tribunal or court; sanctions to be imposed if there is a failure to comply; the composition of the court and the role of the Secretary of State.

26. Hall, Michael (ed.) (1998) *Springfield Inter-Community Development Project: Report of a Series of Seminars*. Newtownabbey, Island Publications.

This brief publication is an edited overview of a series of seminars focusing on anti-social behaviour, interface issues and marching rights. Neil Jarman discusses the contentious issues surrounding parading rights in several different countries, looking at the parades issue from an international perspective. Jarman takes examples of how the parades issue, rights to demonstrate and rights to freedom of assembly are dealt with in the USA, Israel and South Africa, and asserts that although general principles may be drawn from elsewhere, they are always specific to localities. He outlines that when unionists and nationalists in Northern Ireland talk about rights, they are not always necessarily talking about the same thing, which can lead to tension between groups, which often needs to be resolved by third party mediation.

The booklet highlights the USA as a case study, where the right to demonstrate is not restricted in theory, although it often is in practice. The freedom of assembly also provides the right to protest, and Jarman outlines the positive role that has been played by the Community Police Unit in New York, who liase between the parade organisers and the police, and act as intermediaries to attempt to solve any crisis situations through dialogue. In Israel the basic right of assembly was allowed in 1980 with the courts arguing that the main emphasis of the police should not be to stop a demonstration but rather to facilitate it. Both the Israeli and USA examples cited have recourse to the courts in an arbitration capacity, and in Israel there is no right to parade where one wishes and the courts can impose restrictions on a demonstration.

The publication also examines the South African response to demonstrations and clashes focusing on two methods, a monitoring project and a Commission of Inquiry. The role of both of these is said to be very important, as it is suggested that often to try and diffuse situations a third party is needed. There is a recognised right to demonstrate, but with an emphasis on negotiation and flexibility with local dialogue particularly encouraged. The publication explores the history of contentious parades, arguing that every time there is conflict in Northern Ireland, parades have been larger, and concludes by documenting discussion from the floor of the seminars. The safety triangle example of South Africa is outlined as an example of good practice, and the publication contends that if people do not engage in negotiation, they have forfeited their rights.

27. **Hall, Michael (2004)** *Exploring the Marching Issue: Views from Nationalist North Belfast*. **Newtownabbey, Island Publications.**

This publication documents the effects that the marching season has on any emerging political initiatives, and suggests that few people in either community are satisfied with the current situation. The pamphlet attempts to open up a debate on the marching issue, documenting the results of discussions involving community activists from nationalist areas of North Belfast most affected by contentious parades. The publication outlines the view that there was no consensus within the nationalist community as to why they objected to parades, and various reasons for objecting to Loyal Order parades are proposed. These include opposition to the behaviour of those under the influence of alcohol, the 'blue-bag brigade', and the restriction of movement associated with the heavy policing of contentious parades. Some of the participants perceived the Apprentice Boys to be 'better' than the Orange Order, and not all participants were against parades per se, only with ones that went through nationalist areas without prior consultation.

The participants discuss their attempts to engage with the Protestant community and note how disagreement over marches can set back cross-community work by as much as twelve months, with the resulting animosity possibly affecting other interface work. Several participants said that this presented them with a dilemma, on the one hand opposing Orange parades, yet on the other trying to work with Protestant communities. Participants are asked as to why they feel the parades problem has escalated in recent years, and the role of Drumcree in 1996 is seen as critical in inflaming tensions between the communities. The participants' objections to Orange parades include the presence of UDA and UVF flags and their members being present in marches, with some of those involved believing that the whole point in marching is to offend nationalists. There were much less difficulties with small groups of marchers with no music, no banners and no flags.

There were some worries as to how Protestants would receive the document, with a key difficulty believed to be that Catholic opposition to marches is so strong as to bring out most Protestants in unquestioning support of the Loyal Orders. The report concludes with the belief of one participant who felt that despite their differences there were many good Orangemen, and they needed to engage more with working-class Protestants and further assess attitudes within the nationalist community.

28. Hamilton, Michael (2001) Determining the Right to March. *Just News*, Volume 16, Number 6. Belfast, Committee for the Administration of Justice.

This brief paper notes that between January and June 2001 there were forty Parades Commission determinations, over half of which were in Portadown. Hamilton notes that every determination invokes Articles 10 and 11 of the European Convention on Human Rights, and suggests that determinations of the Parades Commission can be evaluated against two of the objectives, which underpinned the Public Processions Act. Hamilton outlines that the first objective of the Act was to introduce a Code of Conduct, and highlights that the Parades Commission's willingness to lift specific restrictions when parade organisers have given assurances of good conduct has been a positive development. The second objective of the Act was to provide alternative criteria by which decisions about parades could be taken, and Hamilton sees this as leading to those who could muster the greatest threat of violence winning. The introduction of the Human Rights Act of 1998 has led to an increasing tendency to cite the likelihood of public disorder in support of decisions. ECHR jurisprudence does not offer clear guidance on what level of public disorder may justify restrictions on peaceful assemblies, or on whether it matters where the threat of disorder emanates.

Hamilton argues that the most unfortunate side effect of the Human Rights Act is that public bodies that have a duty to give effect to convention rights view it as just another hurdle to get over. The challenge facing the Parades Commission is how best to develop a more robust jurisprudence in Northern Ireland based on how to take a clear and principled stand on public order grounds.

29. Hamilton, Michael (2005) Parade Related Protests: is it the 'Taking Part' that Counts? *Just News*, Volume 20, Number 7, July/August. Belfast, Committee for the Administration of Justice.

This short article argues that the extension of the Parades Commission's remit by the Public Processions (Northern Ireland) Order of 2005 to include the power to impose conditions on both parade related protests and supporters of public processions leaves difficult questions on the regulation of protests unanswered. Hamilton notes the problems associated with parade hangers-on, and suggests that the 2005 Public Processions Order gives the Parades Commission power to impose conditions on supporters of a public procession, and that participants do not have to intend to be part of a parade. Hamilton also outlines that the 2005 Order gives the Parades Commission power to impose conditions on protest meetings, but provides no legislative definition of what organising or taking part in a parade is, and makes no distinction between participants and non-participants. The paper cites examples of international law coming into conflict with domestic courts over this issue.

30. Hamilton, Michael (2007) Freedom of Assembly, Consequential Harms and the Rule of Law: Liberty-limiting Principles in the Context of Transition. *Oxford Journal of Legal Studies*, Volume 27, Number 1.

This article explores the concepts of democracy, tolerance and recognition, and evaluates their capacity to generate liberty-limiting principles which advance these ends. Hamilton highlights the tension between the protection of civil liberties and the transitional imperative of democratic consolidation, and seeks to ascertain whether the liberty-limiting principles adopted during transitional phases in societies coming out of conflict should be different from those followed in stable and democratic contexts.

The author contends that the reconstruction of public space in divided societies requires ethical consensus, and discusses the basis for these ethical considerations and whether or not they should be derived from arguments deriving from democracy, tolerance, or recognition. It is suggested that the open-texture of rights language provides a vehicle for building consensus about how best to share public space, and that any consensus will be more resilient if there is a shared understanding of what is the transitional endgame. Hamilton therefore argues that positive recognition of others' position is preferable to mere tolerance.

The article provides background to parade disputes in Northern Ireland, suggesting that there is little consensus about what a human rights approach entails. There is criticism of the often speculative nature of Parades Commission determinations in attempting to work out which parades may cause violence, while the lack of clarity in Parades Commission determinations can create confusion. Hamilton believes that the 1998 Public Processions Act does not tackle the fundamental issues, and that there needs to be vocabulary of rights to generate consensus about the scope of rights which are to be engaged.

31. **Hamilton, Michael; Jarman, Neil and Bryan, Dominic (2001)**
    Parades, Protests and Policing: A Human Rights Framework. **Belfast, Northern Ireland Human Rights Commission.**

This report explores the relevance of international human rights standards to parades and protests, and the policing of those events in Northern Ireland. The authors suggest that European Convention on Human Rights case law, which was fully incorporated into UK law on 2 October 2000, appears to be contradictory, and they explore how these human rights standards impinge upon the freedom of assembly and expression. The document also assesses the significance of international interpretations of disputes around parades for Northern Ireland, focusing on the European Convention on Human Rights and the International Covenant on Civil and Political Rights.

Chapter One *Introduction* provides some background and a brief guide to international standards. Hamilton et al outline that the International Court will give a certain amount of leeway to domestic authorities when determining whether or not a government has fulfilled its obligations, known as the 'margin of appreciation'. The qualifying paragraphs in the ECHR Article 11(2) allow for restrictions to be placed on rights in the interests of national security/public safety, the protection of health or morals and the protection of rights and freedoms of others. The Human Rights Act, which came into UK law in 2000, enables victims of human rights abuses to refer decisions to local courts as opposed to having to go to the European Court, and the Good Friday Agreement of 1998 similarly provided individuals with the opportunity for greater recourse to human rights legislation.

Chapter Two *Parades and Related Protests: A Rights Framework* discusses the right to freedom of peaceful assembly enshrined in Article 11 of the ECHR and Article 21 of the ICCPR. It is noted that if a counter-demonstration becomes violent then the counter-demonstrators have themselves already overstepped the legitimate exercise of the right to freedom of peaceful assembly and should thus forfeit the protection afforded by that right. Following the incorporation of the ECHR into domestic law through the Human Rights Act 1998, courts in Northern Ireland could actively re-interpret those cases that relied heavily upon wide margins granted to national authorities. Route restrictions have been held to be an infringement of the right to peaceful assembly, for the right itself has not been interpreted restrictively.

This chapter examines reasons for restrictions on processions in greater detail. These reasons can include national security or public safety; the prevention of disorder or crime; the message conveyed by a parade; the role of hangers-on; the intentions of the organiser; whether there is to be any related protest; any history of disorder; the potential for disorder elsewhere; the current political climate; whether there is any evidence of steps taken to resolve the dispute and the likely impact of the parade on community relationships. The authors claim that preventing a breakdown in relationships within the community cannot be an aim of the Parades Commission, rather only a factor to be considered. It is argued that although communal consent runs counter to the principles of tolerance and pluralism, there should be efforts to take into account residents' considerations which may be related back to the aim of preventing disorder, and this could fall under the remit of a right to a fair hearing under Article 6 (1) of the ECHR and Article 14 (1) of the ICCPR.

Chapter Three *Affected Individuals and Communities* examines some principles enshrined in international human rights law such as the right to respect for private and family life and peaceful enjoyment of one's possessions under Article 1 of Protocol 1 of the ECHR. The possibility of a 'right to be consulted' has been given some consideration in three judicial review proceedings involving the Parades Commission, and the authors contend that the fact that a parade route has not been changed for many years may give rise to a legitimate expectation on the part of residents in the area that they be consulted before any changes are made.

Chapter Four *Policing Public Assemblies* highlights that the introduction of the Public Processions (Northern Ireland) Act in 1998 removed the power of the police to re-route or impose conditions on parades. This section reviews the general responsibilities of the police with regard to managing public order and then discusses case law of the European Court of Human Rights to consider how this has clarified the role and limitations of the police, before finally addressing the issue of the right to life and the use of force. The European Court has established that while there is a right to peaceful protest, this does not extend to the right to provoke others to violence. This implies that protestors have a responsibility to refrain from actions that might produce a violent reaction from others. In Northern Ireland there were some examples where the police used force to disperse unlawful, but non-violent protest demonstrations such as the Tour of the North in 1996, the Garvaghy Road in 1997 and the Ormeau Road in 1999. The right to life as set out in Article 3 of the Universal Declaration of Human Rights and the ICCPR Article 6 is not unconditional. There is a range of situations in which the deprivation of life will not be regarded as being breached, provided that the use of force was 'no more than absolutely necessary'. This occurs in three situations: in defence of any person from unlawful violence, to affect a lawful arrest or prevent escape and for the purpose of quelling a riot.

The report highlights that decisions taken by the European Court often have given the state much control over decisions pertaining to freedom of assembly and route restrictions are held to be an infringement of the right to peaceful assembly. The publication notes that the policy of communal consent has no basis in international law, and the authors conclude by arguing that the incorporation of the ECHR into UK law opens the possibility of local jurisprudence developing, possibly with cases being brought before the Northern Ireland Court.

32. **Hamilton, Michael and Bryan, Dominic (2006) Deepening Democracy? Dispute System Design and the Mediation of Contested Parades in Northern Ireland.** *Ohio State Journal on Dispute Resolution*, **Volume 22, Number 1.**

Part One *Dispute Resolution as a Procedural Device of Communicative Action* relates dispute system design to theories of democratic dialogue and in particular Habermasian theories of communicative action. The section utilises the concept of 'democratic triangulation' to illustrate the important role that alternative dispute resolution (ADR) mechanisms can play in mediating the relationship between democratic institutions and normative cultural values. The section notes that dispute resolution mechanisms such as the Parades Commission can deepen democracy. In utilising the theory of communicative action, the authors suggest that in the absence of any background consensus, parties will seek to further their own interests strategically rather than attempting to resolve the conflict communicatively.

Bryan and Hamilton adopt the model of 'reflective democracy' in which a deliberative body such as the Parades Commission can produce preferences which are more empathetic, considered and far reaching. A procedural device should facilitate the emergence of background consensus and the reduction of oppositional preferences. The Parades Commission represents an attempt to address longstanding structural inequalities in the public sphere and illustrates the potential capacity of an institution to address entrenched identity-based conflict and deepen the roots of democratic governance.

Part Two *Crisis Consciousness and Parade Disputes in Northern Ireland* documents the background to the Northern Ireland Parades Commission and argues that the Parades Commission demonstrates the contribution that dispute system design can make to the resolution of identity-based conflict. The section contends that parades sustain a sense of locality and territory. The chapter discusses a number of meditative interventions during the mid-1990s outside of the legal framework including local church leaders, business representatives and local politicians among others which encouraged 'forum shopping', where parties participated only in those processes they believed would deliver their strategic goals. The section examines parade disputes from the mid-1980s onwards and documents the role of the RUC in these disputes. The section argues that it is significant that the Parades Commission was designed outside the political system and developed as an exceptional ad hoc reform mechanism. It concludes that the fact that many parades carry an accompanied risk of sectarian violence suggests that at some level the interests of those on the periphery are not yet being adequately articulated through institutional channels.

Part Three *The Parades Commission: Toward Responsive Law* examines the Parades Commission's structure and processes of framing and bargaining. It argues that the independence of the body is paramount, as in this way a regulatory body that incorporates dispute resolution mechanisms and is situated independently between civil society and the institutions of government can serve a mediating role. This triangulation process prevents the new body from being tainted by the legacy of partnership with government, provides a forum for greater civil society involvement in decisions and enables fledgling structures to develop roots. In this sense the Parades Commission needs to be both independent and representative, although the representative nature of the Commission has been challenged three times in the High Court. Bryan and Hamilton suggest that representativeness should be relegated to a secondary consideration and greater attention should be paid to the independence of the body. The authors suggest that institutionalised devices of framing and bargaining can shift disputants from their entrenched positions in relation to one specific issue and by doing so can encourage agreement on other issues. Bryan and Hamilton believe that the Parades Commission largely conforms to Goodin's reflective model of institutional responsiveness, where inclusivity and quality of inputs are important. They claim that procedural transparency can serve to create a situation where parties compete to demonstrate their bona fides. The section contends that there is a perception that the Parades Commission continually moves the goal posts of engagement, which creates a chill factor for some, and the full potential of the Authorised Officers is undermined by their links to the adjudicatory body.

Part Four *Clarifying the Public Interest* returns to the concept of democratic triangulation and analyses the design strengths and weaknesses of the Parades Commission against this. It is argued that the concept of democratic triangulation with ADR mechanisms mediating between state institutions, public policy and cultural values provides a new forum for dialogic intervention, and in this sense the Parades Commission has had some success. There is room for improvement within the Commission's work, particularly in generating greater consensus around underlying interests, values and norms within society.

33. Human Rights Watch/Helsinki (1997) *To Serve Without Favor: Policing, Human Rights and Accountability in Northern Ireland.* New York, Human Rights Watch.

This publication discusses police powers in Northern Ireland, the composition of the Royal Ulster Constabulary, paramilitary policing and punishment attacks, and allegations of collusion between loyalist paramilitaries and the security forces. These issues are considered in depth against the backdrop of the violence of 1996 and it is suggested that during the 1996 disturbance at Drumcree, police actions helped to exacerbate the conflict.

Chapter Four *The Policing of Parades and Marches* focuses on public order legislation in Northern Ireland, particularly the 1987 Public Order (Northern Ireland) Order, and criticises what it sees as the dual role of the police under the 1987 Public Order (Northern Ireland) Order. This leads to the RUC not only making decisions on the conditions of a parade, but also being responsible for enforcing those particular decisions. The authors are critical of this 'wait and see' approach and contend that the exercise of police powers should not simply be a consideration of which side can demonstrate a greater show of force.

The report discusses the Drumcree stand-off in July 1996 and claims that the police made no attempt to stop the large crowd from gathering at Drumcree. Human Rights Watch/Helsinki Watch are also critical of the government's assertion that it was uninvolved in the Chief Constable's decision to initially allow the parade to go ahead and then overturn this initial decision. The authors suggest that no message was conveyed to local residents of the Garvaghy Road area, while claiming that the police response to protestors was heavy handed and involved the use of sectarian language. It is argued that the use of plastic bullets by the RUC came at a time when there was no obvious threat to police; it is suggested that the firing was random and indiscriminate, and the professionality and partiality of the police is questioned. The report argues that the British government should have intervened under public order legislation.

The chapter also addresses events in Derry Londonderry between 11 and 14 July 1996. The authors criticise the behaviour of the RUC and assert that the use of plastic bullets actually led to an increase in the violence. In particular, the report criticises the RUC over events at Altnagelvin hospital when there was alleged harassment and intimidation of victims receiving treatment. It is also critical of the manner of Dermot McShane's death, who was killed by an Army Saracen. The report, although mainly critical of the RUC, does highlight what the authors perceive to be the positive role of the RUC in Dunloy in stopping loyalists attacking nationalists. The authors contend that the RUC conduct on the Lower Ormeau resulted in a 'hemming in' of the local residents in near curfew like conditions.

Human Rights Watch/Helsinki Watch further suggest that there was a disparity in the number of plastic bullets fired at unionist and nationalist protestors, with 662 allegedly fired at unionists and over 5,000 fired at nationalists. It is noted that 1996 was the second highest statistical year for the firing of plastic bullets, with more than 7,294 discharged by the police and army. The report discusses the HMIC Plastic Bullet Review, and contends that the findings indicate not only that the police response to incidents of large scale public disorder was inadequate, but that resources, training, command structure and communications were also ineffective. The authors add that there is a casual attitude to the use of plastic baton rounds amongst some police officers, and that their deployment has the potential to escalate public disorder. The report calls for a total ban on the use of plastic bullets.

The report discusses UK government obligations under international law, particularly the use of force under Section 3 (1) of the Criminal Law (Northern Ireland) Act 1967, and the UN Code of Conduct for Law Enforcement Officials, which dictates that force should only be used when strictly necessary. The report argues that the principle of 'reasonableness', which is the standard for the use of force in Northern Ireland, should be replaced by the standard of 'necessity', which is grounded in international standards and codes of conduct. The authors conclude that where the exercise of the right to free assembly infringes on the rights and freedoms of others, only limitations proportionate to protection of the rights of others can be imposed on the assembly.

34. Irish Parades Emergency Committee (1998) Observors Guidebook. New York, Irish Parades Emergency Committee.

This brief document is a guidebook from an Irish American perspective on the conflict in Northern Ireland aimed at international observers. The issue of consent is a key concept in the publication, and the observer's role is to try and prevent any violence against nationalist protestors, document any human rights abuses and disseminate information from their own perspective on Northern Ireland back in the USA with a view that international observance will get the Orange Order to stop marching. The document lists who is to be observed and what is to be recorded and criticises the RUC, British Army and loyalists. The booklet concludes with some political and cultural dos and don'ts for the observers.

35. Irish Parades Emergency Committee and Brehon Law Society (2005) *Sectarianism on Parade: Orange Parades in Northern Ireland, Summer 2005 International Observors' Report.* New York, Irish Parades Emergency Committee.

This report documents the observations of members of the US based Irish Parades Emergency Committee and the Brehon Law Society at contentious parades in the Ardoyne and Short Strand in Belfast and in Portadown in June and July 2005. While noting that two of the worst flashpoints have been Ardoyne and Short Strand, two reported examples of a positive outcome were at Lower Ormeau and Derry Londonderry where compromise was achieved.

The publication documents the presence of loyalist paramilitary members and symbols at contested parades through a number of photographs, and cites what it believes to be sectarian harassment arising from these parades as violating a key principle of the Good Friday Agreement, namely, 'freedom from sectarian harassment'. The report claims that the parades have seen an increase in loyalist paramilitary flags since 1996, and infers that police or stewards made no attempts to remove them. It is suggested that there should be a refusal to allow parades if paramilitary flags are flown and the British government are accused of parading loyalist paramilitarism through nationalist areas. The booklet notes that the code of conduct required by the Parades Commission includes a ban on paramilitary clothing and flags, on displays of musical instruments with paramilitary markings, on sectarian words or behaviour and that only hymns are to be played at churches. It is contended that the presence of UVF flags at Short Strand and the Albertbridge Road, and particularly those depicting Brian Robinson (ex-UVF), are in direct contravention of the Code of Conduct, as was the playing of sectarian tunes.

The observers specifically document the Springfield Road Whiterock parade in September 2005, and also what the booklet perceives to be the similarities between the 1974 Ulster Workers' Council strike and the 2005 Whiterock riots, which indicate a sense of loyalist anger at their loss of hegemony. The observers claim that the police and army used heavy-handed tactics to 'force' marchers down nationalist areas, and focuses on the Twelfth parade at Ardoyne which resulted in the use of water cannon and plastic bullets by the police. The report subsequently assesses policing and highlights that in the view of the observers, policing has improved, although the authors are critical of the cost of policing parades. They also express concern that prior to 2004 the PSNI did not see 'hangers-on' as falling under the Parades Commission guidelines and restrictions. This has changed however with new legislation from May 2005, and the Parades Commission has the power to impose conditions over any person organizing, taking part in, or supporting a public procession.

It is argued that police conduct in September 2005 has done more to earn credibility with the nationalist community than any other event, and the report concludes that the PSNI must uphold the rule of law, enforce decisions and ban loyalist displays. Similarly, it is argued that the Orange Order need to demonstrate their leadership by ending loyalist paramilitary displays at any of their parades, as the presence of any paramilitary symbols is a direct violation of the Good Friday Agreement.

Other reports on loyalist parades include:

- *Parading Paramilitarism: Conflict in Northern Ireland, Summer 2002 International Observers' Report.* New York, Irish Parades Emergency Committee.
- *Marching and Disorder: Conflict in Northern Ireland, Summer 2003 International Observers' Report.* New York, Irish Parades Emergency Committee.
- *Law and Lawlessness: Orange Parades in Northern Ireland Summer 2004 International Observers' Report.* New York, Irish Parades Emergency Committee.

36. Jarman, Neil (1993) Intersecting Belfast. In Bender, Barbara (ed.) *Landscape: Politics and Perspectives.* Oxford, Berg.

This chapter suggests that terms such as 'Protestant' and 'Catholic' obscure internal ruptures in which the voices of the paramilitaries and their political organisations maintain an essentially working-class critique of their respective mainstream cultures. The author contends that these voices emanate in code and speak from the walls of working-class estates and the music of parades and practices of young people.

The author provides a brief description of the early years of the Troubles and the population movements between 1969-1976. This exacerbated existing segregation practices and led to the development of interface communities. The role of the security forces in Belfast in restructuring the urban environment is discussed, as the building of army posts, cameras, and observation posts in defensive planning indicated a willingness to settle for an acceptable level of violence. This control and containment imposed on working-class estates is contrasted with attempts to normalise the situation in the commercial centre of Belfast.

Jarman examines gable wall murals as the preserve of working class areas and until recently, the preserve of the loyalist community. After the hunger strikes of 1981, freshly painted republican murals became a catalyst to loyalist painters, and the aftermath saw a plethora of new loyalist murals in working class areas. Many of the paramilitary murals are painted next to or among Williamite and Orange emblems, and thus shifted the orientation of Orange symbols away from themes of civil and religious liberties and glorification of past victories to focus on the legitimacy of armed defence, and the chapter proposes that this has been a transformation in the meaning of murals.

Jarman states that the emphasis for much of this mural painting comes from the approach of one or other commemorative marches. A brief history of the Orange Order is provided, and Jarman examines the Belfast parade in the city centre. He refers to the Twelfth as a day of celebration of 300 years of Protestant dominance and nationalist exclusion from the city itself. The march through Belfast itself is said to reassert Protestant power over that space and also the primacy of religious values over the commercial and administrative. For loyalists, a key feature in asserting their power in a Protestant state is the right to march where they will and when they will. Jarman claims that the parades are both a statement about Protestant supremacy and also an act of reunification in the face of the fragmented geography of Belfast. When individual members parade it is to be interpreted as an embodied geography. Jarman concludes that the working-class population are challenging and redefining the norms of the traditional authorities of the middle-class, Orange Order and the Catholic Church.

37. Jarman, Neil (1997) *Material Conflicts: Parades and Visual Displays in Northern Ireland.* **Oxford, Berg.**

This study analyses some of the ways and means by which past events are remembered in Northern Ireland, and focuses on numerous commemorative parades within both unionist and nationalist traditions. In particular the study considers the relationship between these acts of remembrance and celebrations with the violence of the Troubles. The study explores the conflict between collective memories and how a collective or social memory is generated and maintained.

Chapter Two *A Custom Established 1690 - 1790* traces the development of parading in the 1770s focusing on the Volunteer movement. In this era, parading became established as an instrument of political action, when there was also a new development in the culture of parading with ceremonial, commemorative and political demands all becoming inseparably intertwined. By 1793 when the Volunteers had disbanded, public parades with music and flags were transformed into an established feature of political life, creating unified national identities, both unionist and nationalist. The chapter suggests that parades were soon to become the medium that gave visible form to demands of the emerging Protestant middle-class as they sought to translate their increasing wealth into political capital, and to this extent they were greatly helped by the social, economic and political climate of the eighteenth century.

Chapter Three *Riotous Assemblies: 1796–1850* charts the conflict in Armagh between the Catholic Defenders and the Peep O'Day boys as leading to the establishment of the Orange Order in 1795, while outlining that it was the Ribbonmen who established the custom of parading in the Catholic community. The flourishing of street decorations and arches in the 1810s and 1820s occurred at a time when there was increased sectarian tension over O'Connell's campaigns for Catholic rights. The 1820s and 1830s saw a general escalation in the culture of parading and an increase in sectarian clashes. It was during this era, Jarman asserts, that Orangemen reacted to O'Connell's campaign by marching more often, in more places, and with more people. This was because in times of political uncertainty, parading helped to build connections and intensify differences with the 'other' side. The chapter concludes that parades gradually became one of the major expressions of lower-class socio-economic political aspirations as sectarianism emerged, openly celebrated by commemorative parades by the 1840s.

Chapter Four *Parading Identity: 1870–1968* notes that after 1872 and the lifting of the Party Processions Act, parading resumed with increased support of the 'respectable' middle classes held against the backdrop of political demands, and both the Twelfth and St. Patrick's Day parades became closely drawn into the wider political process. It was in this era that the practice of using 'the field' for political speeches at Orange parades developed, and with both the Ancient Order of Hibernians and the Orange Order becoming more 'respectable', by the 1890s sectarian rioting at parades was no longer as widespread as before. The chapter argues that Orange displays and parades were no longer seen as embarrassing by the Ulster Protestant middle-class; they were rather seen as key to maintaining their power base and parading became refocused as a vehicle to display unionism. Parades grew to an enormous size, with 100,000 taking part in Belfast in 1926 watched by 50,000 spectators. The section concludes that the civil rights parades in the late 1960s confronted the belief that parading was largely the prerogative of loyalists, claiming that the civil rights parades became a visible symbol of the Catholic/nationalist challenge to the state.

Chapter Five *The Glorious Twelfth* focuses on the role the celebrations play in creating a sense of community among the Protestants of Belfast, with the parades reaffirming the Protestant position and at the same time antagonising many nationalists. Jarman provides some background on the preparations for the Twelfth in the Sandy Row area of South Belfast, and the role of the parade in marking out the unity of four distinct geographical communities in the Sandy Row district and in providing a sense of allegiance to the local community. The main Belfast Twelfth parade provides for a ritual reunification of the dispersed Protestant communities of Belfast and allows them to claim authority of the city centre, marking the city of Belfast as Protestant.

Chapter Six *The Endless Parade* discusses other Loyal Order organisations such as the Royal Black Institution and the Apprentice Boys, and highlights the difference between the shorter, rural, quieter and more religious Black parades with Orange Order parades. Jarman suggests that the large number of Orange parades (2,500 in 1995) held is in part due to the decentralised nature of the organisation, and he proposes several reasons to account for the increase in parades over the years. These include decentralisation, a sense of threat from the Anglo-Irish Agreement in 1985 and the growth of a new type of 'Blood and Thunder' bands. The discrepancy between the numbers of loyalist and nationalist parades is related to the broader political history of Ireland and the power imbalance in the north, with loyalists expecting to march where and when they will in their country, while regarding nationalist parades as threats to public order. Jarman states that the opportunity to demand and to exercise the right to march is a symbol of the distribution of political power in Northern Ireland. The section concludes that the earliest signs of the parades dispute were in the early 1980s in Castlewellan and Downpatrick, and then Portadown in 1985 and 1986. The role of residents' groups in the 1990s illustrates the continued symbolic and political significance of parading and the difficulty of balancing those rights with the rights of the protestors.

Chapter Seven *Our Day Will Come – Parading Irish Nationalism* looks at nationalist parading history, and documents Ancient Order of Hibernians parades during the Troubles, which although generally peaceful affairs, saw some violent clashes after the hunger strikes and the Anglo-Irish Agreement, such as that at Draperstown in 1980 and Magherafelt in 1984. Jarman notes that republicans have five main annual parades, which include the birth of Wolfe Tone, the Easter Rising, Bloody Sunday, the 1981 hunger strikes and the Internment commemorations. In Belfast the main nationalist commemorations have been confined to West Belfast historically, and only in 1993 for the first time was an Internment rally held at Belfast City Hall. It is suggested that loyalist parades are essentially triumphal expressions of collective determination and strength in unity, while republican parades show resolve in defeat and a determination to carry on the fight.

Chapter Eight *Trust in God, but keep your powder dry* discusses the Orange Order, Black Institution and marching bands. It provides an analysis based on images on several hundred banners photographed at parades between 1990-1996 focusing on the image of King William. Jarman suggests that the majority of images at parades are of King William or religious imagery, and he outlines that the banners of the Royal Black Institution are more biblical in nature than those of the Orange Order. The image of King Billy is that of an abstract, symbolic figure, which is removed from any specific historical context, usually depicted on a white horse, which is a symbol of the purity of the heroic subject.

Chapter Nine *A Nation Once Again* outlines how republicans used banners less until 1995, when this changed due to the campaigning nature of their politics. The chapter examines the banners of the Ancient Order of Hibernians which usually depict more diverse messages, with the most common images those of St. Patrick, the Madonna and the Pope. The female personification of Erin is often depicted on the banners and there is a greater emphasis on heroic, secular resistance than on Orange banners. The dominant theme running through the images is the importance of religion in forging and maintaining Irish national identity. The Irish National Foresters use Erin to invoke a sense of Irishness based on a history of self-justified actions rather than one legitimated by reference to the Catholic Church. They are more inclined to highlight the role of more radical Protestants such as Henry Joy McCracken. The banner displays by the supporters of Orange and Green obscure much of the more obvious support for the gun within the commemoration of a heroic and glorious past.

Chapter Ten *At the Going Down of the Sun* outlines that loyalist murals declined in numbers in the early years of the Troubles, but loyalist painters were stimulated once again by the 1981 republican murals painted in the aftermath of the hunger strikes. This chapter discusses how paramilitary groups use murals to try and situate themselves within unionist tradition and legitimise themselves. The previously established images of King Billy murals are now adjacent to paramilitary gunmen and highlight the emergent working class critique of Orangeism. Jarman uses the example of South Belfast to highlight how murals are used to express distinct local identities, such as the difference between Ulster Defence Association/Ulster Freedom Fighters murals in Sandy Row and Ulster Volunteer Force murals of the Village area. He argues that this territorial division has as much to do with music as it does with guns and highlights the sometimes ambiguous relationship between some marching bands and loyalist paramilitary groups.

Chapter Eleven *Hungering for Peace* asserts that religious, Gaelic and historical symbols were forged together with internationalist icons to create a new republican iconography that would later be reproduced on nationalist streets. The author notes that many recent memorial murals are symbolically linked each year by band parades held on the anniversaries of prominent paramilitary figures' deaths, and claims that a distinct loyalist marching season somewhat similar to the established republican practice of small, local parades to honour their dead is starting to emerge.

Chapter Twelve *In Conclusion* states that, although from the late seventeenth century the form of parades appears to have changed little, the detail and meaning have changed considerably. Jarman links parading to politics and asserts that parading is shaped by the broader political world. In the nineteenth century, parading and commemorations were of major importance in helping mould the sectarian divide within the north of Ireland and once established, have been instrumental in perpetuating divisions. The extensive and repetitive practice of parading and the visual displays associated with parades have become the most prominent ways and means that the people of Northern Ireland use to construct their collective memories and also to display their differences. Parades have multiple meanings and the Troubles have been prominent in expanding the practice of parading, with 'traditional' parades expanding particularly after the two ceasefires of 1994. Jarman concludes that the process of parading in Ireland has been a central custom and one that has helped constitute antagonistic collective commemorations for Catholics and Protestants. The parades are usually symbolically predicated on the rhetoric of war and constitute difference by helping to construct competing identities, which are now solidified as 'traditional'. Parading is the cultural medium through which people can generalise about the 'other' community. Parades are perhaps distinctive of specific Northern Irish culture and will remain a distinctive means of displaying faith for the foreseeable future.

38. Jarman, Neil (1998) Material of Culture, Fabric of Identity. In Miller, Daniel (ed.) *Material Cultures: Why Some Things Matter.* London, UCL Press.

This essay examines the history of banners as social objects, and shows how banners have become the visible and material repository of the Orange tradition. Jarman contends that traditional practices are assumed to have a greater validity than non-traditional practices and that tradition is assumed to bestow rights and obligations. The first part of the essay traces aspects of the social history of the custom of using banners and other forms of social display, and focuses on the textile industry and the close relationship between the economic importance of linen and its significance as a symbolic medium. The author notes the link between Protestant prosperity in the growing industrial area of Belfast and the rise in the linen industry. The cloth, he argues, provides the economic basis for the Protestant community and reaffirms the close link with Great Britain.

The Orange Order by the early nineteenth century was widely established throughout rural Ulster and the Order consolidated and extended the custom of parading en masse with elaborate visual displays. By the late 1880s, these rural traditions had been transformed by two developments, the emergence of Home Rule and the professionalization of banner painting. Jarman notes the role of George Tutill in oil painting on silk in England in the 1860s, and the role of William Bridgett in Ireland who produced an array of historical, political and biblical designs. The years between 1886 and 1914 saw mostly Williamite, Lutheran and Siege of Derry images depicted on the banners, but subsequent to this period there was a rapid increase in the number of local figures such as William Johnston. Jarman argues this is because Ulster Protestant identity became more identified with Ireland and Ulster than with Britain, with many UVF and Somme banners after 1916. It is outlined that these banners as objects have become bearers of 'traditional' values. The chapter outlines that the majority of present day banners were established by 1930 and that the overall conservatism of the banners reflects the centrality of history and sense of tradition within the aims and ideals of the Orange Institution itself.

39. Jarman, Neil (1999) **Commemorating 1916, Celebrating Difference: Parading and Painting in Belfast**. In Forty, Adrian and Küchler, Suzanne (eds.) *Materializing Cultures: The Art of Forgetting*. Oxford, Berg.

This essay explores how long established customs of parading with music and banners and painting elaborate wall murals combine to maintain extensive social popular memory. The chapter also compares and contrasts nationalist and unionist practices and suggests that both the Battle of the Somme and the Easter Rising helped consolidate contrasting notions of collective identity in a period of political upheaval. The Somme was immediately drawn into the existing structure of popular expressions of

Orange and unionist identity and succeeded in broadening unionist iconography. Jarman argues that the Somme wreath laying ceremony and parade in July is an act of mimesis that re-enacts the departure of the Ulster Volunteers to World War One. Although the parade is almost entirely male dominated, the importance of women is acknowledged, as they cheer and encourage the departing volunteers and wait on their return. The parade itself reaffirms the validity of the cause and confirms the declared willingness of the present generation to fight again if necessary. The focus is on heroic bravery rather than the severity of the casualties suffered. Jarman asserts that while the Williamite campaign is commemorative through its leaders, social memory of the Somme dissolves individuality into the single identity of the Ulster Division, with all of the battles condensed into the memory of the Somme.

The advent of the Troubles saw major changes in the relationship between the marching bands and the Orange Order particularly in urban areas, and the bands tend to commemorate local tradition, ignoring Orange Order guidelines. The essay explores the phenomenon of nationalist parades and outlines that they have never been as numerous as Orange parades in Northern Ireland, they have never been welcomed by the state, and that they have been largely restricted to areas defined as nationalist. The Easter parade to Milltown is described in detail and Jarman argues that while the Orange Order has managed to retain diverse groupings within a single commemorative event, the nationalist movement has tended to fragment.

The chapter explores the differences between Orange and Green parades, highlighting a substantial difference in structure and form in the parades, with unionist parades being more militaristic in style. Jarman contrasts the unionist optimistic march to war with the more solemn republican funeral parade, asserting that while Orange parades are essentially triumphal expressions of a collective determination and a celebration of strength in unity and brotherhood, republicans commemorate the continued resolve in defeat and the determination to carry on the fight. The author traces the origins of the loyalist style of parading to the paramilitary traditions of the eighteenth century Volunteer movement, whose customs were redefined in the combative sectarian politics of the nineteenth century. This is contrasted with republicans, who draw heavily on a funeral procession tradition of the Ribbonmen and Freemasons, and Jarman compares the 1861 funeral procession of T.B. McManus and O'Donovan Rossa's funeral in 1815 to Bobby Sands' mass funeral procession in 1981. This traditional method has been the most consistent means of mobilizing public support and while military victory structures loyalist parades, republicans tend to mourn their dead. The Somme commemorations are more collective in emphasis, given that Protestant authority remains invested in the community, while republicans tend to highlight the sacrifice of specific individuals.

The essay concludes with the view that social memories do not draw on some unquestioned mass of empirical facts, but rather that they are the product of sifting through the confusion of the past for evidence that serves to substantiate existing beliefs. These public commemorations help to convert those selective details into unquestionable history, and the fact that parades in Ireland sustain and extend popular memory has the effect of sustaining antagonism between Catholic and Protestants.

40. Jarman, Neil (1999) Regulating Rights and Managing Public Order: Parade Disputes and the Peace Process, 1995-1998. *Fordham International Law Journal*, Volume 22, Number 4.

This essay opens by contending that the Good Friday Agreement contains no references to parades, marches, processions or demonstrations, and yet over the past four years parades disputes have come to dominate the political agenda. Jarman explores the problems that have emerged over the right to parade since 1994 and provides a brief review of the significance of parades in Ireland before summarizing the background to the current disputes. The chapter also reviews the attempts to resolve the issue, varying from formal British and Irish government measures, the Independent Review of Parades and Marches, changes to parading legislation and the formation of a Parades Commission with legal powers.

The essay explores some legal controls on parades and marches, suggesting that in the initial stages, the problem of disputes over parades was regarded as a relatively minor matter with dialogue facilitated at a local level. Jarman describes the history of the gradual development of public order legislation from the 1922 Civil Authorities (Special Powers) Act (Northern Ireland) to the Public Order (Northern Ireland) Order of 1987, and documents violence related to public order in England in the early 1980s and violence in Northern Ireland in 1985. This led to the 1987 Public Order (Northern Ireland) Order which removed the clause exempting 'traditional' parades from giving a period of notice.

The policing of parade disputes is addressed, and while the police always cited the Public Order (Northern Ireland) Order of 1987, Jarman suggests that the ability to exercise the right to march in the past has tended to be contingent on the ability to mobilize a significant threat of force rather than a moral or legal claim to notions of human rights. Jarman states that this is an inappropriate means of deciding civil rights and raises concerns about the consistency and criteria of this approach and the transparency of decision-making. In 1996, the decision to overturn a previous decision and allow an Orange Order march down the Garvaghy Road after three days of loyalist riots saw the RUC give in to the threat of violence and undermined their credibility in both the nationalist and unionist communities.

The essay briefly discusses the North Report and argues that it gave too much prominence to concerns for public order and too much emphasis was placed on the significance of traditional parades. In relation to the Drumcree dispute in 1998, Jarman highlights the failure of local politicians to move away from a sectarian position, and he concludes that the approach of Drumcree 1999 is a threat to the peace process, particularly given its symbolic significance to the unionist community.

41. **Jarman, Neil (2000) For God and Ulster: Blood and Thunder Bands and Loyalist Political Culture. In Fraser, T.G. (ed.)** *The Irish Parading Tradition: Following the Drum.* **Basingstoke, Macmillan.**

This chapter discusses loyalist marching bands within wider loyalist political culture, and suggests that membership of a marching band provides status in one's own community. Jarman argues that the marching bands occupy an ambiguous position within the unionist community in that they are essentially an ingredient of loyalist political culture, yet exist largely outside the control of the Loyal Orders while simultaneously challenging the Loyal Orders in their parades. Jarman alleges that the music of the marching bands can raise tensions between the two communities, as was the case in Derry Londonderry in 1995. Loyal Order parades are seen as complex occasions, and are successful as they have largely managed to avoid the factionalism which has characterised Protestant denominations and political parties. The author highlights the role of symbolic displays in defining collective identity and notes the role they play in providing for a temporary coalition of interests. To this extent, Jarman contends that the symbolic displays are successful due to their ambiguity. Desmond Bell's study of youth culture is suggested to be limited, as it understands the bands as a localised expression of loyalist youth sub-culture, rather than something more fully embedded within the wider unionist culture.

The 'Blood and Thunder' bands are largely a by-product of the Troubles. Until the 1970s, band culture was incorporated within the broader realm of Orangeism. It is now the case that most bands have no formal connection to the Orange Order and Jarman proposes three reasons for this. Firstly, that working-class disenchantment led to younger elements abandoning the Orange Order. Secondly, that the perceived inability of the Orange Order to defend Ulster led many to look towards the UVF and UDA. Finally, that the Orange Order became generally irrelevant to the interests of working-class youth. It is contended that many marching bands have a close relationship to the UVF/Red Hand Commando and some more recent events suggest that the nature of this relationship may be more than symbolic. Jarman highlights some examples of the close ties between the bands and paramilitaries, and highlights that they draw on the same sections of the community for support as do the paramilitaries. Unlike Bell, Jarman believes that the links between certain marching bands and loyalist paramilitaries can be real, and certainly more than mere bravado. For many, 'Blood and Thunder' bands are the public face of loyalist paramilitarism.

Jarman concludes that the violent, percussive sound of the drum ignores spatial boundaries and carries the claims of the Protestant community to all parts of Northern Ireland, and that the rise of the marching bands has signalled the decline in power and importance of the Orange Order within the Protestant community.

42. Jarman, Neil (2003) From Outrage to Apathy? The Disputes over Parades, 1995-2003. *Global Review of Ethnopolitics*, Volume 3, Number 1.

This essay opens by exploring the Drumcree parade dispute of 1996 and suggests that it remained unresolved and raised tension each summer as July approached. The widespread rioting that followed Drumcree in 1996 is contrasted with the situation in 2003 when, within an hour of the Orangemen leaving Drumcree Church, the area was deserted with no widespread protests or violence. This article analyses the reasons for the different responses to the restrictions on the Drumcree Church parade in 1996 and 2003, reviews the changing contexts around the disputes over parades and discusses the changing regime for managing the disputes.

Jarman charts the beginning of the current disputes over parades to the period immediately after the 1994 paramilitary ceasefires, and outlines the contrasting positions taken by nationalist residents' groups and the

Loyal Orders over the right to parade. These positions varied between viewing parades as a legitimate expression of culture or as triumphal expressions of domination. The essay explores the view of the Loyal Orders that nationalist residents' groups were mainly fronts for Sinn Féin and republicans, and contends that the objections to parades were more widespread within the Catholic and nationalist population and actually predated the ceasefires. The essay cites surveys of public attitudes to suggest that, even for many within the Protestant community, there was considerable ambivalence if not hostility towards parades. The decrease in the number of disputes over parades has been the result of a number of factors relating both to changes in the way that the disputes and general threats to public order are now managed, and also to changes in the wider political context. The paper suggests that no single act or area of activity is responsible for the transition from the extreme violence of 1996 to the virtual non-event of 2003. There was rather a diverse number of factors including government policy, legislative changes, the creation of the Parades Commission, policing practices and the changing wider political context.

Jarman documents responses to the formation of the Parades Commission, outlining that while nationalists were broadly supportive, unionists were generally suspicious and hostile to it. The Parades Commission has been effective to some extent with local solutions due to the considerable local knowledge and contacts of the Authorised Officers. More recently, the informal contacts have led to some sort of solution to the disputes on the Ormeau Road by enabling Orangemen to create a new route covering part of the 'traditional' route, but which avoids passing along the contentious section of the Ormeau Road. Jarman asserts that while parades still remain a persistent problem, the work of the Parades Commission in six years has made a significant impact on reducing the likelihood for violence. Part of the process of imposing a new sense of order on parades and parading organisations has been in encouraging an understanding that exercising rights includes recognising social responsibility. The main problem many people have with parades is the disruption that they cause, the paramilitary displays and the unruly behaviour associated with the events. At many parades an informal system of stewarding crowds has been developed by people close to paramilitaries to try and control the 'blue-bag brigade'.

Two main factors have influenced the reduction of public protests against parades. First, once people realised that a determination would not be changed on the day through the threat of force, there was no longer any compelling reason to mobilise large crowds to try to influence decisions.

Second, as the organisers came to accept that the police would implement a determination whether they organised a public protest or not, there was less impetus to appear on the streets and to mobilise bodies in support. There has been a greater willingness to rely on debate to determine whether and how a parade should take place and what form the protest should take, rather than attempting to mobilise the threat of force to make the police act against the other side. From 1996 onwards, local human rights groups sent people to disputed parades to monitor the policing of events and there was considerable criticism of the scale of the force used by the police in responding to public disorder in 1996 and 1997.

According to Jarman, the attempts to diffuse the tensions over parades have drawn upon a variety of conflict resolution approaches. Until recently, these approaches focused on negotiations and bargaining amongst political elites. More recently, these official, public negotiations have often been supplemented by unofficial, informal and exploratory diplomacy that have operated outside of official channels, often facilitated by trusted third parties such as international NGOs, churches and academics. Track 3 approaches, which involve grass-roots actors, are at present in the ascendancy, and the essay argues that collectively these different approaches have been important in helping to reduce tensions and prevent outbreaks of widespread violence on the scale of 1996.

The controversy over parades has been largely resolved through a blend of the relatively successful introduction of a new regime for managing disputes, combined with an extensive variety of local engagement involving a range of actors. The author concludes that one key problem has been that the wider issue of acknowledging the importance of cultural, ritual and symbolic events and processes within the construction and maintenance of ethnic identities has tended to be seen as a subsidiary and minor issue. The Belfast/Good Friday Agreement has been relatively successful in producing a blueprint for the structure for the future government of Northern Ireland, but it carefully avoided those issues that underpin the fundamentalism of the two main ethnic communities and helped to sustain the sectarian divisions of the society. These issues have to be addressed if Northern Ireland is to move beyond ethnic division, competition and fear.

43. **Jarman, Neil and Bryan, Dominic (1996)** *Parade and Protest: A Discussion of Parading Disputes in Northern Ireland.* **Coleraine, Centre for the Study of Conflict.**

This publication analyses the background to parade disputes in 1995, considers the attitudes of those involved and suggests proposals to resolve or improve the situation. Jarman and Bryan provide a typology of parading, outlining nine different types of parade and also provide a chronology of the main parades from Easter to December. The report documents a ten-year overview of parades between 1985 and 1995, and highlights that rerouting has been a consistent problem for the Royal Ulster Constabulary. The authors contend that these ten years gave rise to two distinctive features that require explanation, first an increase in the number of parades and second the large difference in numbers between loyalist and republican parades. Jarman and Bryan speculate that the increase in loyalist parades has been due to small feeder parades and competitive band parades. Since 1994 and the ceasefires, parades have become a prominent and highly visible means of displaying and mobilising behind traditional public demands.

The publication examines the major disputes involving parades in 1995 and divides 1995 into four distinct parading periods using two main sources: the local press and the authors' own personal attendance. They argue that there is a need to take a decision to allow, ban or reroute a parade earlier as it reduces the potential for conflict. They conclude that RUC tactics in Derry Londonderry were a blow to community relations and again there was a failure to make the decision public until the very last minute. The publication suggests that there are two main points in understanding the geography of the disputes. Firstly, that they usually occur in segregated areas where working class Protestants have moved out to the suburbs and the Catholic community is consolidated in the inner city. Secondly, the Loyal Orders' insistence on marching 'traditional' routes without any acknowledgement of these demographic changes that have taken place. The authors contend that the symbolism of Derry Londonderry is very important in the Protestant psyche, each parade that is challenged is a symbolic threat to Protestant security and the unionist position, and each parade which passes a nationalist area is a restatement of the dominance of the Protestant community.

The report also analyses different perceptions from the groups involved in the disputes and examines the role of the police and the media. The parades are an attempt to assert a general identity but also to reassert a specific local identity. The perception of 'tradition' in parades masks that they are part of a present political situation and part of the changes that are taking place. Many within the Orange Institution are disenchanted with the leadership and specifically with the weakened ability of senior members to influence local political situations. Jarman and Bryan highlight that new factions within unionism need to legitimate themselves by drawing upon the past, by utilising symbols and going on parade. Nationalists, however, often perceive the parades to be triumphalist, an attempt to reassert territorial dominance and a symbol of oppression requiring a massive police presence. In defending parades, the RUC are seen as working with the Loyal Orders. Many loyalists alternatively see the parades as part of their 'tradition', as oppositional to a 'pan-nationalist' front, and perceive any compromise as a defeat. The authors question the validity of this 'tradition' argument espoused by Orange Order, and argue that many in the Loyal Orders misunderstand the roots of nationalist objections to their parades.

The section discusses options raised for possible resolutions to the disputes. Jarman and Bryan claim that the control of demonstrations is not specific to Northern Ireland as in England there has been control over football fans and the Notting Hill carnival for many years. This is said to raise issues of civil rights, and they ask the question at what point should the rights of the individual to express themselves be seen as secondary to the more general good of the community? The publication discusses seven different issues that need to be approached in looking at parades which include a need for a formal mechanism to resolve disputes, and that clarification and a longer time frame need to be allowed for mediation.

The authors revise a Lower Ormeau Concerned Community proposal that in order for a parade to proceed, it must have prior consent. They argue that this should not be the case, although the feelings of residents do play an important role in considerations. There is a need for dialogue and compromise, and absolute rights of veto are not helpful. The publication calls for the establishment of a Parades Commission and suggests that judgements should be made on the issue of public behaviour at marches, as the situation of 'parading without responsibility' cannot continue indefinitely. Jarman and Bryan suggest four key points: everyone has the right to parade; this should be balanced by residents' rights; the Loyal Orders need to be held accountable and responsible for what takes place and there needs to be an arbitration period.

The document concludes that most parades are peaceful and cause little offence; the long-term aim is not to prevent parades, but to encourage a political environment where civil rights are respected and political expression can take place without inconveniencing others.

44. Jarman, Neil and Bryan, Dominic (1998) *From Riots to Rights: Nationalist Parades in the North of Ireland. Coleraine,* Centre for the Study of Conflict.

This report examines the history of Irish nationalist and republican parades and commemorative events. The study involved surveying newspaper reports and other published material to reveal some generalised tendencies. The report claims that in order to understand the role played by parades, one must first examine relationships of political power, given that the existence of 'traditional' parades is directly related to the political power that the respective communities have held.

Chapter One *Diverse Roots, Varied Customs* details the long history of parades in Ireland, which are believed to be at the very least 500 years old, but were extended towards the end of the eighteenth century. With Catholics restricted by penal laws, often funeral processions were used as a show of strength to those in power. The authors explore the history of the Volunteer movement of 1778 to 1792, and suggest that the modern practice of parading is to be found in the histories of the Orange Order, the Ribbonmen and the Freemasons between the 1790s and 1860s.

Chapter Two *Parading for Home Rule* examines the role of William Johnston in repealing the Party Processions Act in 1871. Subsequently, Jarman and Bryan contend that parading between 1872 and 1914 flourished as part of nationalist political culture in the north, growing steadily in size, scale and significance. Within nationalism, parading was never taken up with the same purpose as among Orangemen, and was more linked to the broader political agenda than developing of its own accord. The chapter discusses the role of the Ancient Order of Hibernians, the Irish National Foresters and the Gaelic League, and contends that Irish nationalist parades were never really accepted in the north by a large part of the Protestant community. They were at best tolerated in areas where nationalists were in the numerical majority, but were often opposed and physically confronted. The chapter asserts that the nationalist struggle to parade throughout the 1870s and 1880s would become a key feature in building and sustaining momentum for Home Rule. As nationalists sought to increase their rights to parade for Home Rule, Orangemen often physically challenged them, usually by holding a counter-demonstration, and frequently the authorities took the easy way out and banned both for fear of public disorder. The general policy was that if there was a possibility of loyalist violence, then nationalist parades should be cancelled or restricted.

Chapter Three *Culture and Commemorations* suggests that parading was both widespread and a popular activity from 1872 through to the 1900s, with nationalists ready to confront opposition by Protestants. From the mid-1880s, physical opposition from Protestants appears to have decreased as the authorities became more willing to uphold nationalist rights. The chapter documents the decline in nationalist support for nationalist parades which would appear to be the result of internal dynamics within the Catholic community, with three major factors including the opposition to parades from the Catholic Church, the lack of a body to coordinate demonstrations, and the wider relationship between parading and the political campaign for Home Rule ending. The chapter concludes by detailing the background of the Ancient Order of Hibernians and the Irish National Foresters claiming that the former introduced a more strongly sectarian and more Catholic outlook to the movement, and was less involved in overt political structures.

Chapter Four *Special Powers in Northern Ireland* discusses the formation of the state of Northern Ireland in 1920. During this period unionist control of the legislature and Protestant domination of the police force was reflected in the ability of the Protestant community to hold parades and demonstrations and the inability of nationalists and republicans to do the same. The chapter claims that organised public expressions of opposition to unionist control of Northern Ireland involved constitutional Irish nationalism, the Irish Republican movement, and Trade Unions and left-wing action. Jarman and Bryan document incidents of attacks on nationalist demonstrations including in June 1932 on their return from the Eucharistic Congress in Dublin, and the 1935 riots in Belfast which left eight people dead. The forces of the state allowed public political displays by constitutional nationalists as long as they did not transgress into areas perceived as Protestant, although by this time the Ancient Order of Hibernians was in decline and being eclipsed by the republican movement.

Chapter Five *A Golden Era?* analyses the post-war period in Northern Ireland, with the period up until the mid-1960s fondly remembered as a relatively trouble free time, when Catholics would watch parades. The authors believe that this period, one of low IRA activity after the unsuccessful border campaign finished in 1962, led to greater confidence amongst unionists and a more relaxed and less confrontational Twelfth. The chapter discusses the Public Order Act (Northern Ireland) 1951 and Flags and Emblems (Display) Act (Northern Ireland) of 1954, which effectively exempted the Loyal Orders from having to give prior notification of a parade. The police reaction to republican displays in the

1950s is examined, and Jarman and Bryan assert that due to the relationship of the state with public political displays through legislation and the actions of the police, it was relatively easy for politicians to engineer incidents by threatening demonstrations or counter-demonstrations.

Chapter Six *You Can March – Can Others?* traces the demonstrations of the civil rights movement, which most directly challenged the rights of public political expression. These civil rights marches directly challenged state control upon political expression, which opposed unionist power, but the period saw the decline of the Ancient Order of Hibernians and from 1971 to 1975 they banned their own members from taking part in parades. The chapter highlights that Sinn Féin utilise four key annual republican commemorations; the Easter Rising, Bloody Sunday, hunger strikes and Internment, and Jarman and Bryan reflect upon the dynamics and difference within the nationalist/republican community that these events can create. They discuss the role of Easter commemorations, which physically challenge the state, highlighting paramilitary strength versus the police. Despite problems in the 1980s and riots in 1981, since the late 1980s there has been a reduction in the number of disturbances associated with anniversaries.

Chapter Seven *The Right to March* assesses the significance of the return to Direct Rule, and the chapter argues that coupled with the introduction of new Public Order legislation in 1987, the RUC in the 1980s were tougher on Orange parades than they had been previously. Jarman and Bryan contend that since 1994 there has been a move back to civil rights and claims to political expression in the public sphere. Since the mid-1980s there has been a gradual extension of rights of nationalists to use town and city centres due to political campaigns by republicans to extend demonstration routes, a shift in the attitude of state institutions, and increased leniency from unionists towards the less overtly political Ancient Order of Hibernians. The 1993 Internment Rally with 15,000 republican supporters at Belfast City Hall highlights how access to public space to nationalists has increased.

The chapter charts the increase in nationalist opposition to loyalist parades in the 1990s and comments that concern over parades on the Ormeau Road did not begin in 1992. There were disturbances in 1969-1972; in fact concern over the right to march has been a facet of community relations for many years. The authors discuss two consequences of the 1994 ceasefire, in that it allowed constitutional nationalists and republicans to work together in areas such as the

Garvaghy Road, while the loyalist ceasefire gave residents more confidence to be seen to oppose events in public. Throughout much of the 1970s and the 1980s the military nature of opposition had limited any form of communal campaigns for or against parades, but the shift in the mid-1980s from more military to political approaches opened up a space which would lead with the ceasefires in 1994 to parades being much more assertively challenged. The section concludes that since the early 1970s the forces of the state have become more tolerant of republican political expression and less tolerant towards certain elements of loyalist political expression.

Chapter Eight *Some Conclusions* discusses some of the rights of public political expression in legal terms, and argues that there is no absolute right to hold a parade or a demonstration. Jarman and Bryan argue that everyone should have equal access to parades and demonstrations and contend that there is a need to put in place a process through which judgements can be made. They believe that there is a need to develop a vibrant culture of civil rights, with a prerequisite being that the Irish and British governments commit to legislative and policing reform.

Chapter Nine *Some Recommendations* examines how the ceasefires and the peace process changed the political environment and proposes some reforms. Jarman and Bryan assert that the concept of 'tradition' has not existed in a political vacuum, but rather has developed through relations of power. They are therefore critical of the inclusion in the Public Processions (Northern Ireland) Act 1998 in Section 8.6e of the 'desirability of allowing a procession customarily held along a particular route'. They also recommend the development of a full Bill of Rights and a judicial system capable of arbitrating those rights, and propose the establishment of a Parades Commission to make determinations on parades decisions as they suggest that it is not wise for the police to make decisions over rights to public political expression. The authors state that reform of the RUC is needed urgently and minority communities need to be protected, as public order decisions in effect leave the majority population in an area effectively retaining a veto over the actions of the minority. The report also recommends that those organising events should also police themselves, and improved training is needed for stewards, while there needs to be greater understanding with reference to public political expression. The study concludes with the belief that a political accommodation will not necessarily mean the end to political conflict, and that political differences will have to be managed without resorting to physical force.

45. Jarman, Neil; Bryan, Dominic; Caleyron, Nathalie and de Rosa, Ciro (1998) *Politics in Public: Freedom of Assembly and the Right to Protest, A Comparative Analysis.* Belfast, Democratic Dialogue.

This publication examines the way in which public political expression is facilitated and looks at a number of issues that impinge upon public political expression. These include the judgement of toleration and the judgement of rights based upon tradition and custom. The study also compares legislation dealing with and the practice of managing parades and protests in Northern Ireland with elsewhere, including among others the USA, South Africa and Israel.

Part One *Northern Ireland* discusses parades and protests in 1996 and 1997. This section argues that the organisation of parades on a nightly basis in Belfast in early July 1996 provides a striking example of when the right to public political protest can threaten serious disruption to the life of communities. The research discusses this in the context of the findings of the North Report, which outlined a key finding as giving consideration to the wider impact of a parade on relationships within the community. Jarman et al see the problems over parades as driven by dynamic events surrounding disputes, political pressure and external pressures. The authors note the case of the Apprentice Boys' parade on Lower Ormeau in April 1996 and several parades in Derry Londonderry during the same year. The authors discuss some differences with these two examples and others, such as the fact that they both involve large nationalist communities and small Protestant communities. There was also said to be the negative influence of alcohol, and in Derry Londonderry in particular the behaviour of outsiders not from the area was said to have affected community relationships.

Part Two *The Right To Demonstrate: Case Studies of Law and Practice* argues that parades, demonstrations, protests and marches are a fundamental part of the democratic process and almost inevitably a source of conflict given that to demonstrate or protest in favour of something means to protest or demonstrate against something else. The Chapter deals with the legislative background to restricting processions in England, and charts the rise of the Notting Hill carnival, highlighting five areas of relevance for parades in Northern Ireland. These include liaison, police/organiser co-ordination, stewarding, residents and resources.

The situation in Scotland is noted as being legally different to the situation in England and Wales, as the council or local authority makes determinations on parades as opposed to the police. The authors briefly discuss the history and development of Orangeism in Scotland and contend that alcohol has been an even bigger problem in Scotland than in Northern Ireland. The authors comment that the Orange Order in Scotland tackled paramilitarism in two ways, firstly through band membership of an association, which effectively operates a band registration scheme, and secondly through a detailed band contract specifying what behaviour is and is not acceptable.

The chapter also discusses the cases of the Republic of Ireland, France, Italy, the USA, Canada, Israel and South Africa. Using France as an example, the publication raises the question of whether it is acceptable for one section of society to decide what opinions deserve the right to be expressed. The authors also conclude that the lowering of social conflict in Italy in the 1980s allowed for a culture of mediation to develop, and that the willingness to ban or disperse parades depends on the prevailing political climate. In the United States, the role of community police officers in the St. Patrick's Day parade along Fifth Avenue is seen as an element of good practice, as they act as intermediaries keeping the lines of communication open. In Canada, parades are not allowed to disrupt the city's commercial life too much, while the right to freedom of assembly in Israel has not been equally open to all groups, with Palestinian Israelis often denied the right.

The section highlights the use of independent monitors at public events. These monitors acted as intermediaries between rival groups, and between demonstrators and the police. Other monitoring groups included a wide range of organisations within civil society and also the African National Congress and the Inkatha Freedom Party. Many groups were mixed, with both locals and outsiders from the ANC and IFP, and the training of volunteers was seen as vital in reducing the threat of violence. Jarman et al contend that the reform of the South African police highlights that it is possible to undertake a thorough and largely acceptable reform of an institution completely identified with the previous regime. The authors stress the point that in South Africa, new legislation acknowledges the inherent political nature of many public gatherings with an interlocking structure of the decision making process in which organisations within civil society, the police and civil authorities are all equally responsible.

Part Three *General Principles* highlights a number of issues that recur when dealing with the issue of demonstrating and the section proposes a series of principles representing current best practice, which may be used in Northern Ireland. These include:

1. Provision of constitutional guarantees.
2. Clear legal framework.
3. Recognition of a right to demonstrate by all.
4. Limited recognition of 'tradition'.
5. Advance notification for events and of any restrictions.
6. Clear parameters for imposing constraints.
7. A right to appeal any constraints.
8. A right to protest but not to prevent public events.
9. Provocative demonstrations allowed in city centres, with more sensitivity in residential areas.
10. Sensitive policing with limited recourse to force.
11. Greater use of stewards and monitors.
12. Control of alcohol.

46. **Jarman, Neil and Bryan, Dominic (2000) Stewarding Crowds and Managing Public Safety:** *Developing a Co-ordinated Policy for Northern Ireland.* **Belfast, Community Development Centre.**

This report is a development of one section of a previous report related to the monitoring of public order, and focuses on the role of stewards at events. The report defines stewarding as an attempt by organisers to manage an event by controlling behaviour of those attending as participants, spectators or customers. The publication discusses the roles and responsibilities of stewards, and highlights two primary areas of concern: the reasons for internal control of an event and the managing of spectators, and also the interface between the organisation and the wider public. The report outlines that stewards can provide a policing function, although they may often have strained relations with the police, particularly in the context of Northern Ireland. Jarman and Bryan contend that due to the links between stewards and event organisers, they are not usually suitable for dealing with some outside relationships.

It is suggested that at many parades in Northern Ireland, stewarding is well meaning but ineffective, at others it is appalling. This is due to the fact that stewards are not often visible, are inappropriate, and may have little communication and poor relations with the police. The publication concludes that there is a general consensus that stewarding is useful in promoting responsible management of the public-private interface, but highlights that there is no agreement over common standards or integrated training programmes. The report stresses a need to develop a co-ordinated policy to stewarding, with organisers recognising their responsibility. Presently there is no compulsion on organisers to provide appropriately trained stewards. There are two proposed ways to support this, by introducing legislation requiring it, and by encouraging a voluntary process whereby groups and individuals understand the importance of good stewarding. The study suggests that the Assembly needs to take the lead on this issue and that a new co-ordinated and streamlined approach to developing steward training and development is needed.

47. **Jarman, Neil and Bryan, Dominic (2000) Green Parades in an Orange State: Nationalist and Republican Commemorations and Demonstrations from Partition to the Troubles, 1920-1970. In Fraser, T.G. (ed.)** *The Irish Parading Tradition: Following the Drum.* **Basingstoke, Macmillan.**

This chapter argues that the right of nationalists to demonstrate during the years of the Stormont government was contingent on the local balance of demography and power. The expansion of the Orange parading 'tradition' and lack of a comparable green 'tradition' has been closely linked to the differentials of power within the northern state. Jarman and Bryan discuss loyalist opposition to Ancient Order of Hibernians (AOH) parades in loyalist areas. It is noted that 1935 saw the worst sectarian violence in Belfast, with nine days of riots leading to the deaths of seven Protestants and 2,000 Catholics having to flee their homes. This was against the backdrop of an escalation in Orange parades in the 1930s and the introduction of the Public Order Act of 1936.

The authors document the post-war period as one that is strongly remembered by unionists as trouble free, and they attribute this general belief with a greater confidence among unionists in this era allowing for more relaxed events. Jarman and Bryan argue that it is precisely this generation brought up in the 1950s and 1960s who would later become involved in the disputes of the 1980s and who would inevitably contrast those later experiences with memories of previous, happier times. The chapter suggests that despite parade disputes in the 1960s, community relations were possibly the best they had been in the twentieth century. It was in this period, the authors note, that Ian Paisley would utilise his skills within the sphere of public political procession. Jarman and Bryan argue that it is easy for hard-line politicians to engineer incidents by threatening demonstrations or counter demonstrations, due to the relationship of the state with public political displays in legislation and policing terms. The chapter finishes with a description of the events leading to the Battle of the Bogside on the 12 July 1969, and concludes that what had started as a non-violent campaign that questioned the control of public space by unionism had developed into an armed challenge to the existence of the state.

48. Jeffrey, Keith (2000) Parades, Police and Government in Northern Ireland, 1922-1969. In Fraser, T.G. (ed.) *The Irish Parading Tradition: Following the Drum.* Basingstoke, Macmillan.

This chapter analyses the relationship between parades, the police and government in Northern Ireland. The chapter opens by discussing the legislative enactments of the Stormont regime, the Civil Authorities (Special Powers) Act of 1922, and the 1951 Public Order Act superseding this. Jeffrey asserts that between 1922 and 1950 there were 91 proclamations prohibiting meetings under regulation 4 of the Special Powers Act, with the author noting three occasions when loyalist parades were halted during the wars, notably the Twelfth of July in 1932, 1935 and 1938.

Jeffrey argues that the loyalist tactic of counter-demonstrations was relatively unused during the wars, but re-emerged in 1948 when the government policy on nationalist demonstrations had shifted. He contends that the political risks taken by government ministers who offended Orangemen were demonstrated in 1953 with the general election, when the Minister of Home Affairs Brian Maginess in County Down almost lost his seat to an independent unionist. The author notes that the Orange Order position was that any trouble at their parades was the responsibility of those that caused it and not themselves as the parade organisers, and that even if a demonstration came from outside the nationalist spectrum such as one by a trade union, it was treated like a nationalist parade. The chapter concludes that the traditional methods used from 1922 in policing public processions were no longer effective by the outbreak of the Troubles.

49. Jones, David; Kane, James; Wallace, Robert; Sloan, Douglas and Courtney, Brian (1996) *The Orange Citadel: A History of Orangeism in Portadown District.* Portadown, Portadown Cultural Heritage Committee.

This publication provides a history of Orangeism in the town of Portadown from the perspective of the Portadown Cultural Heritage Committee. The authors document the background to the formation of the Orange Order in 1795, and they outline Twelfth celebrations over the years in Portadown itself. The right to march along 'traditional' routes is seen as key, and the publication contends that the Orange Order are not out to provoke anyone when they march, but rather they march to enjoy and celebrate their distinctive culture and heritage. The report is critical of what it perceives to be heavy-handed policing of the Twelfth in Portadown over the years, and states that 1873 saw the first recorded violence directed against Orangemen in the Tunnel area of the town. The authors discuss the home rule crises of the late nineteenth and early twentieth century, arguing that the growth of Irish nationalism in this period gave an increasing role to the Orange Order as defenders of the Protestant community.

The post-war era is seen as a 'Golden Age for Orangeism', one when there was no controversy over traditional parade routes, and it is suggested that it was the onset of the Troubles that saw a growing resentment of traditional Orange parades passing through the Obins street area of the town. The rerouting of the parade in 1985 and 1986 is seen as perhaps the most traumatic period in the Orange Order's history, while the events of the early 1990s are viewed as more peaceful and optimistic than those a decade previously. The publication concludes with a discussion of the events at Drumcree in 1995.

50. Kelly, Gráinne (ed.) (1998) *Mediation in Practice: A Report of the Art of Mediation Project.* Derry Londonderry, INCORE.

This booklet contains two sections, with the first section focusing on the Art of Mediation Workshop and recording the views of three individuals involved in mediation. The second part of the report provides a detailed study of mediation in relation to parades in Northern Ireland in the summer of 1997. The research seeks to highlight the potential for local dialogue and the positive contribution that mediators can bring. It outlines trust as a key factor in mediation, with Northern Ireland approaches to mediation more flexible than the traditional model. It is highlighted that mediators are not always professional and impartial, they can have authority within a certain section of the community. The section contains six case studies of mediation, with the first focusing on Bellaghy. The booklet describes the events of 10 July 1996 when the Royal Ulster Constabulary forcibly removed protestors against an Apprentice Boys march. The chapter outlines that an agreement was reached between the Bellaghy Concerned Residents and the Royal Black Institution at a time of high tensions after a Loyalist Volunteer Force (LVF) murder in the area, and highlights a number of problems facing the protagonists which included the sheer number of parades in the village and Sinn Féin's influence on the local residents' group.

The second case study focuses specifically on Dunloy, where a deal was rejected due to the influence of the 'Spirit of Drumcree' group led by Joel Patton. The report suggests that despite the failure, both sides agreed principles held by all citizens, including respect, equality, freedom of movement and the common good. Case study three examines the situation in Dromore where difficulties emerged over tensions from the situation in Drumcree. Small-scale disturbances in 1996 had led to attempts in 1997 to avoid a repeat of the violence, with church leaders facilitating a meeting. The section documents the impact of poor media reporting and misinformation in heightening tensions. One other problem highlighted was that with the structure of the Orange Order being very autonomous, it was often very difficult for local Orange leaders to have the authority to come to a final decision.

The fourth case study focuses on Newtownbutler, while case study five is of Derry Londonderry with the problems there beginning in 1995 with the collapse of an agreement between the Apprentice Boys and the Bogside Residents' Group. The issue of linkages to other disputes appeared to be a key problem in Derry Londonderry. The final case study looks at the situation on the Ormeau Road, and the report highlights the influence that the presence of a Ballynafeigh Orange Lodge banner at the Drumcree stand-off had on relations between the local Orange Lodge and nationalist residents.

The section proceeds to discuss the challenges to the processing of a dispute, such as the connections to the wider political situation, and examines the decision making powers of the Loyal Orders, where representatives are 'first among equals'. The section finishes with a set of guidelines and encourages voluntary mediation processes, with mediation facilitated by a third party and never being imposed. This encourages long-term processes, which can maintain local agreements where possible, as these tend to be longer lasting. There is also a need to engage the wider community through an increase in single identity work through education, while there also needs to be a clarification of the role of the Parades Commission. The publication suggests that it does not seem to be advisable for mediation and arbitration roles to be performed by the same body, as local voluntary mediation is believed to be more effective. The booklet concludes with a summary of three papers from an international conference in November 1997, on Israel/Palestine, Sri Lanka and the United Nations and provides a comparative analysis of the differences in approaches.

51. Kennaway, Brian (2006) *The Orange Order: A Tradition Betrayed.* London, Methuen.

This book considers whether the Orange Institution at the beginning of the twenty-first century is a true manifestation of historical and traditional Orangeism. Kennaway in essence suggests that it is not, and that the Order has drifted away from its core values of love for God, faith in Christ, the Bible and tolerance of others' religious beliefs. Kennaway discusses the establishment of the Orange Order and suggests that Orangeism itself is a broad philosophical concept embracing the great principles of the sixteenth century Reformation. He refutes allegations of sectarianism and anti-Catholicism, which have plagued the Order since its foundation, and argues that the Canadian Order whereby one is allowed to marry a Catholic is a more accurate reflection of original Irish Orangeism than its Irish counterpart. He notes that the Order's leadership is now drawn from more working-class elements as opposed to the aristocratic and business classes of before, and that the Order is no longer the thing to join if you want to 'get on in society'. He contrasts the early years of the Orange Institution and the clear thinking of the leadership with the modern 'tunnel vision', which equates Orangeism exclusively with the Ulster-Scots tradition. Kennaway believes that sectional interest, separation and sectarianism stand in opposition to authentic Orangeism.

The book looks at whether the Orange Institution is a religious organisation with a political element, or a political organisation with a religious element, and argues that initially the Order was primarily religious. In recent years there has been a subtle shift away from defining the Order in primarily religious terms and it has become a cultural movement. The religious nature of the Institution is said to have been compromised by the Drumcree stand-offs, and the author asserts that contemporary Orangeism reflects a less 'religious' Protestantism than at its formation. The book refers to past membership of the Order requiring respectability and discipline, but claims that from the mid-twentieth century onwards there has been a question of discipline relating to Orange Order members involved in political violence. The book notes some examples of a failure of the Order to distance itself from paramilitarism and states that this behaviour contradicted the words and basis of the Institution. He is also critical of contentious Orange parades escorted past flashpoint areas by leaders of loyalist paramilitary organisations. He is critical of the lack of disciplinary action taken against members involved in violence and highlights the contradiction in words and deed of the Orange leadership who claimed that actions would be taken against those individuals found to be paramilitary members. In 1998 he notes, eight members of the local Orange lodge were charged with criminal offences and yet none were disciplined.

Parading is outlined as a key feature of Orangeism, and Kennaway contends that there is an inextricable link between parading and Orangeism as distinct from the Orange Institution. Despite this, he claims that the bands of today are too aggressive and are the factor that most expose the duplicity and inertia of the Institution. The parade needs to be well led by a respectable band, as the public response is very different from one led by a 'Blood and Thunder' band. Kennaway sees 1985 as the year in which parades became a defining issue for the Orange Order. The situation in 1995 and 1996 at Drumcree is discussed, and the author feels that the blocking of the roads in 1996 by Orangemen and their supporters was blatant hypocrisy by those attempting to walk along another road.

Kennaway believes that the Order should take into account demographic changes that have occurred along their 'traditional' routes, and highlights that the 1998 Belfast/Good Friday Agreement made matters worse, and he is critical of the roles of both Harold Gracey and David Jones. He outlines 1998 as the worst year in the history of the Orange Institution, and a time when parading had become the raison d'etre of the Orange Order. The Order, he argues, had alienated many within the Protestant community as the Orange leadership were seen to have capitulated to the hardliners. The book contends that contrary to assumptions, parading is not central to the Orange Order's ideals, and that the conflict in recent years over parades has been at the same time a reason why some people have joined and others have left the Institution. The increasing alienation of Protestants means that parades provide a public display of unity. Kennaway is critical of the Orange leadership's stance at Drumcree and claims that they must be held responsible for the violent events that unfolded. He argues that the Institution itself created the Parades Commission by their inability to reach an accommodation.

The author sees the Institution's present weakness as increasing after the debate on the Good Friday Agreement, and contends that the Order has now shifted away gradually from its core values. Orange Order members' behaviour at Drumcree is seen as one of intolerance, and Kennaway believes that the Institution has come to represent a very narrow view of Protestantism and that the weak and ineffective leadership which has blighted the Institution for years is ruining the Orange Order from within.

52. Larsen, Sidsel Saugestad (1982) The Two Sides of the House: Identity and Social Organisation in Kilbroney, Northern Ireland. In Cohen, Anthony P. (ed.) *Belonging: Identity and Social Organisation in British Rural Cultures.* Manchester, Manchester University Press.

The aim of this chapter is to describe and analyse the basic forms of social organisation in 'Kilbroney', an anonymised town in Northern Ireland, as they occur in everyday life. The chapter suggests that despite the appearance of a single town on the surface, there are in fact two Kilbroneys. The author tries to explain how Catholics and Protestants have attempted to learn to live with the conflict by avoiding interaction with each other in a very ritualised and systematic fashion. Larsen argues that the expression and maintenance of ethnic boundaries is key in Northern Ireland, and highlights that one can see and hear this division expressed through colours, objects and tunes. The chapter describes how these divisions manifest themselves in the town by describing daily life in a cul-de-sac off the main street. The author describes many of the actions that take place here as ones of avoidance, in terms of conversation and in terms of contact with members of the other group. She suggests that songs and music are widely used in Northern Ireland to communicate group membership by recounting the stories of famous battles and those who lost their lives for a righteous cause. The marches of the local Orange Orders and their nationalist counterparts celebrate these causes in the working-class areas of the town. Boundaries are maintained physically in the form of segregated territories and activities such as parading.

53. Larsen, Sidsel Saugestad (1982) The Glorious Twelfth: the Politics of Legitimation in Kilbroney. In Cohen, Anthony P. (ed.) *Belonging: Identity and Social Organisation in British Rural Cultures.* Manchester, Manchester University Press.

This essay is essentially a piece of ethnographic based research based on an anonymised area of Northern Ireland named 'Kilbroney' which the author uses as a case study. The author describes the scene in the area in the build up to the Twelfth, the bands practising, music, church services and so on. She discusses the framework for the Twelfth of July, including the preparations, and particularly the distinguishing of outsiders as different. Larsen gives a short description of the Twelfth day itself, the participants, the dress, the bands, bannerettes, bunting and the flags, and focuses on the religious imagery of Protestant heritage. The author states that our understanding of basic social categories and social processes in Northern Ireland may be enhanced by observing how people relate their customary mode of behaviour to the setting constituted by the Twelfth of July. Larsen asserts that the Twelfth event, being a ritual, constitutes communication at different levels and is aimed at different audiences. The article highlights that there are two categories of audience listening to the message, the Catholic population and the British public. One of the main objectives of the Twelfth event is to clarify the Orange Order's position in relation to the Catholic population, considered to be hostile to its values. This restricted code has a very different significance for an audience outside the relationship.

The chapter then considers in more depth the communication between the participants, briefly outlining the Order's rise and fall, and rise again with the threat of home rule in the late nineteenth century. The author acknowledges the cross-class alliance between political leadership and followers and discusses the political function of the Order in Ireland as well as its ideological basis. The events of the Battle of the Boyne are seen as key, with the potency of the Order lying in the linkage of an organisation with political structure. Here, Larsen suggests that the 'myths' subsequently legitimise the current order, stating that the concept of 'self-defence' links the present order to the mythical past.

Larsen then discusses the role of the followers in this process, claiming that the fictitious prelude to the chapter highlights 'common' Protestant values, such as cleanliness, order, management of property, and these are implicitly contrasted with perceived negative qualities of Catholics of laziness and neglect of one's property. She asserts that this same sense of community solidarity is repeated from the Twelfth platform itself, with an assertion that the history of the Protestant population has been to defend their 'values' previously won through struggle, with an emphasis on group solidarity. The essay addresses the role of the British audience, which is believed to represent the same 'values' that the Protestants of the north share. Larsen explores the opening of a gap in the relationship resulting from the demise of the Stormont regime and reintroduction of direct rule. Therefore the Orange state is seen as under threat from two sides, internal Catholic opposition and opposition from England.

The change in relations between Protestants and Catholics in the summer months at the height of the marching season is assessed, and Larsen highlights how Catholics perceive the event differently. They do not see the event as a show of solidarity espousing common values, but rather as a massive demonstration of control of territory, with the Twelfth a demonstration of Protestant power, and with the presence of politicians only reaffirming this belief. The celebration demonstrates that Kilbroney is a 'Protestant place' with the Protestants in a majority and that the processions and marches are a means of asserting control over that territory. The essay concludes with the view that what is 'glorious' is also 'repressive' in that there are no interactions between the parties and therefore no changing of opposing positions, particularly since there is often little recognition of the legitimacy of the 'other' side's position. Larsen concludes that there is little change in the social relations that these ritual events communicate and no dynamic for change in the codes used for this communication.

54. Loftus, Belinda (1994) *Mirrors: Orange and Green.* Dundrum, Picture Press.

This publication looks at traditional Orange and Green political symbolism and contains a collection of photographs of the Twelfth of July, Orange symbols and nationalist and republican iconography. The author contends that the Twelfth celebrations cannot be understood without decoding the layers of meaning given to their individual symbols and the changes in their overall role and functions. The publication documents the history of Orange lilies, lambeg drums, arches, Orange sashes and banners among other symbols, and suggests that there are two main messages conveyed by these emblems on sashes and banners. Firstly, they denote the hierarchical structure of grades and degrees; secondly, they depict Orangemen as akin to the Israelites in the Old Testament as God's chosen people. Loftus also claims that the carrying of the Bible and sword in Orange parades was adapted from Masonic practice, and the Orange resort to religious parades in the nineteenth century was also encouraged by the increasing emphasis on Anglican and Presbyterian unity in Ulster in opposition to nationalist mass movements.

Orange parades have remained a remarkably resilient form of political demonstration, the strength of which partly lies in their ability to gloss over the impotence which many unionists in Northern Ireland feel in the face of republicanism. The Orange symbols' emphasis on ritualised challenge and quasi-military self-defence can diffuse these feelings of impotence, while their stress on both individuality and unity glosses over fragmentation. In essence, Loftus asserts that Orangemen march to show the united front of Protestantism. The increase in the number of loyalist parades since the 1970s is the result of both the rapid growth in the number of young loyalist marching bands and the continuing commitment to Orange parades as a way of challenging Catholics. The publication contends that the marching bands point to the continuing strengths of the Orange Order and its symbolism, and the author notes the history of and layers of meaning attributed to Orange symbolism.

In terms of Green symbolism, Loftus examines the meaning of Irish symbols such as the harp, the shamrock and tricolour flag among others. The Irish use of green flags is said to date from the mid-seventeenth century. This section documents the development of the harp, shamrock, Irish wolfhound and round tower as national emblems of Ireland against a backdrop of political events of the nineteenth century. It provides background to the Ancient Order of Hibernians in the United States, and argues that their simple forms of religious and Masonic imagery were absorbed from such previous nationalist organisations as the Defenders and Ribbonmen. The author discusses the meanings of the nineteenth century green displays, and claims that it was not until after 1872 and the repeal of the Party Processions Act that Ulster witnessed mass green parades of the AOH and Irish National Foresters among others.

Loftus describes nationalist displays since 1968 and notes that despite the massive 1969 Belfast St. Patrick's Day parade, parades in other areas after this time had mixed fortunes. Some nationalist displays such as those in Armagh and Down from the mid-1990s became more cross-community, while others attracted republican displays. The imagery employed in Northern Ireland's nationalist processions since 1968 derives from historical action and interaction as well as from specific, narrow symbolic traditions and the pressure of political events. Loftus notes that the military nature of much of the green imagery employed in Northern Ireland today derives not simply from the Celtic emphasis on warfare, but also from successive Irish rebellions, the impact of widespread jingoism on Irish republicans, internal conflicts after 1968 and a desire to win international publicity.

The publication concludes with a small section on shared traditions and contends that both Orange and Green imagery are formed from layers of meaning. The numerical dominance of the unionist community in this area and the political stance of its members made it difficult for nationalists to construct such public, political imagery as their counterparts, and instead encouraged them to develop private emblems situated in the privacy of the home or the countryside.

See also: Loftus, Belinda (1990) *Mirrors: William III and Mother Ireland.* Dundrum, Picture Press.

55. Lucy, Gordon (1996) *Stand-off! Drumcree: July 1995 and 1996.* **Lurgan, Ulster Society.**

This publication discusses the traditions of Orange parades from the perspective of the Orange Order itself, and argues that parades are very much part of the Order's tradition and heritage, and a link to the 'Glorious Revolution'. The booklet offers an account of three days during the Drumcree stand-off in 1995 and contains a series of black and white and colour photographs depicting the scene in and around the church at Drumcree Hill.

Lucy suggests that traditional routes are not chosen to cause any offence to nationalists, and contends that the prevention of a peaceful parade is an attack on the culture of a people and a denial of basic civil liberties. He argues that the threat to public order comes from protestors and not parades themselves, and states that the tension surrounding the proposed Drumcree parade was generated by those who opposed the parades. The author accuses residents' groups of using a threat to disrupt public order as an effective tactic to get parades stopped. Criticism is aimed at the Lower Ormeau Concerned Community whom it is believed are merely a front for Sinn Féin and the IRA.

The booklet moves on to document the perceived significance of Drumcree, and highlights the impact that the British-Irish Framework Document had on playing on unionist fears. The author mentions a series of concessions to Sinn Féin, which include the ending of the playing of the British national anthem at Queen's University graduation ceremonies, the lack of IRA decommissioning and continuing IRA punishment attacks. Lucy believes that these factors had the stated effect of mobilising middle-class support for the Orangemen of Portadown, which had not been the case since the disturbances of 1985-1986. The author argues that the unionist response at Drumcree was greatly influenced by the events of 1985 in Portadown, and according to Lucy, unionists and Orangemen were determined that a decade later there would be no repeat of the humiliation of the mid 1980s. He states that the Order had a surge in members after the crisis, with fifty new members in Portadown alone, the largest influx of members since after the Second World War.

The publication states that although the Loyal Orders have a right to march, they should be sensitive to their Catholic neighbours, and the author then moves on to deal with the situation in 1996 with regards to the Drumcree parade. He suggests that the ban of the parade was politically expedient and that, although violence did occur, this was not the fault of the Orange Order. The book contains some media excerpts from political commentators on the situation at Drumcree, most attempting to understand the mindset of the Orangemen in 1996. The booklet concludes that the frustration of Orangemen and unionists resulting from a series of events such as the Framework Document, the Canary Wharf bomb, the appointment of George Mitchell and the pushing of decommissioning further down the agenda were responsible for the events at Drumcree in July 1996.

56. Lucy, Gordon and McClure, Elaine (eds.) (1997) *The Twelfth: What it Means to Me.* Lurgan, Ulster Society.

This publication is a compilation of contributions from fifty individuals on their opinions of The Twelfth. The authors outline that the events of July 1995 and 1996 at Drumcree in Portadown highlight that there are a range of different perspectives on Orangeism, both inside and outside Northern Ireland. The book aims to promote greater debate and improved understanding of the Twelfth itself. The book provides some childhood recollections, for some a defence of the Orange Order, while others provide a critique of the Twelfth itself. The publication documents a wide array of divergent opinion on the Twelfth from individuals such as Ian Adamson, Jonathan Bardon, Ian Paisley Jr, Brid Rogers and Chris Ryder to name a few.

Several contributors document what the Twelfth means to them in terms of their identity, and most particularly their faith. The contributions contain some historical reference to the Boyne and other major events connected to the Twelfth, the importance of the eleventh night growing up in a Protestant area, the sense of belonging to a local community, the complexity of the Twelfth as an event, and the difference between rural and urban parades. One contributor suggests that the reason that Orangemen parade is that they feel their territory is under threat, as is their way of life, and that they are simply proclaiming their loyalty in a public way.

Other contributors are more critical of the Twelfth as an event, with one noting the impact of Drumcree in 1996 on the nationalist psyche, and another contributor suggests that one of the purposes of the parades is to annoy and antagonise Catholics. Some contributors note that they await the marching season with both anticipation and dread, and several individuals believe that the issue of forcing parades through an area where they are not wanted is counter-productive to unionism. One contributor suggests that parades in the divided society that is Northern Ireland reflect the nature of the state, and from a nationalist perspective become a symbol and a celebration of domination and triumphalism, of the victory of unionism over nationalism. The tradition argument is seen as one which relates to a tradition based on an inequality of power as well as one which ignores demographic change.

57. McAuley, Imelda (1998) Reforming the Law on Contentious Parades in Northern Ireland. *Public Law*, 44-56.

This document focuses on the Drumcree dispute of 1996 and discusses the key recommendations of the North Report, which was established in the aftermath of violence associated with parades. McAuley welcomes the establishment of the Parades Commission, but outlines that the adjudicatory role of the body may come into conflict with its conciliatory role. McAuley believes that the Parades Commission may face difficulties, and questions how much authority the body will have if those who do not agree with the body's determinations do not abide by the decisions. The fact that the police can also trigger a review of a decision by the Secretary of State could be perceived by some as the police still retaining a role in the decision making over parades and could detract from the Commission's legitimacy. This combination of decision making by the police and the Parades Commission could prove to be problematic.

She asserts that the main difficulty facing the Parades Commission will be in its application of the criteria in clause 7 (6) of the 1998 Public Processions Bill, and the difficulty inherent in balancing the weight attached to the possible impact of a parade with the desirability of allowing a 'customarily' held parade. The article states that the Parades Commission is not in real terms in a better position than the police with regards to decision making on contentious parades, and the value of freedom of assembly should be carefully considered to inform decisions.

The paper concludes that the Public Processions Bill provides a new approach to parades regulation in Northern Ireland and is an improvement on the 1987 Public Order (Northern Ireland) Order. McAuley concludes that North and subsequent legislation did not fully address how to weigh up competing rights claims. Despite this, the paper acknowledges that the North Report and Public Processions Bill is still a significant first step and a prototype for marching seasons elsewhere.

58. Miller, Deborah J. (2004) Walking the Queens Highway: Ideology and Cultural Landscape in Northern Ireland. Unpublished PhD Thesis, Louisiana State University.

This study documents the types of symbolism prevalent in Northern Irish landscapes and the meanings attributed to them. The study compares two communities in relation to their Twelfth of July parades, Coleraine and Portadown. For each community, Miller examines the parading landscape, parade routing through neighbourhoods, displays of political symbolism along the route and within the parade, participant, spectator and protestor behaviour, and finally the security presence.

The study discusses theories relating to material and symbolic culture and cultural construction in Northern Ireland and draws on Carl Sauer's 'The Morphology of Landscape', which argued that both culture and landscape provide contexts for human activity. Miller highlights that in Northern Ireland marching and mural painting are primary resources for conveying meaning, and that parades define cultural identity in spatial terms by mapping symbolically important routes within the cultural landscape, which then 'trigger potent memories'. The thesis suggests that residents of Portadown create their cultural landscape for several purposes, which include historical reminders, political statements, warnings, territorial markings, and forms of either resistance or domination.

The relatively peaceful parade in Coleraine with its lack of 'Kick the Pope' bands is contrasted with the situation in Portadown, as in Portadown parades are seen as more aggressive, serving to maintain the divide which exists in the town. The author believes that they also serve to assert the rights of Protestants over Catholics there. It is argued that the Coleraine parade, with a closer mix in terms of community background within the town, is more conciliatory, while at the same time Coleraine is much further away from areas that have traditionally suffered more political violence. It is documented that during the years 1968-1993, thirty eight people are listed to have been killed in Portadown compared to twelve in Coleraine.

Miller essentially views the parade in the Garvaghy Road area as a struggle for territory, power and political legitimacy. She suggests that when a community feels disregarded and disrespected, they are intolerant of another community parading their ideology through their space. Miller concludes that the future of parading depends on mutual respect and understanding from both communities.

59. Montgomery, Graham and Witten, Richard (1995) *The Order on Parade*. Belfast, Grand Orange Lodge of Ireland.

This booklet was produced by the Orange Order with the stated intent of better informing people of the nature of the Orange Institution. The booklet claims that it offers a different opinion from the nationalist view that parades are essentially triumphalist and a threat, and rather focuses on the Orange Order's emphasis on a sense of tradition and the link to past generations as vital elements to the parading tradition. The document provides a brief overview of the Twelfth of July celebrations and charts the history of the Order beginning in the late eighteenth century, contending that the Orange Order is primarily religious in nature and that parades are a statement of their religious beliefs.

Montgomery and Witton claim that Order parades are not meant to offend, but recognise that they can offend due to demographic changes. They hope that both communities can support parades in a spirit of tolerance and parity of esteem. They do note however the complaints that people have about the Orange Order with regards to music, flags, shouting, alcohol and 'hangers-on'. It is suggested that opposition to parades is not new, as prior disturbances occurred at Orange Parades in the nineteenth century.

The publication moves on to discuss the future for the Orange Order, highlighting that since 1986 all bands have had to sign a 'band contract' of good behaviour called 'Conditions of Engagement', which contains eleven clauses. The authors cite examples of bands barred from parades for carrying offensive flags to show that they are taking a proactive stance against this sort of behaviour, and state that quite often band parades are mistaken for Orange parades.

It is argued that the rerouting and the banning of parades is a deliberate attack on the Protestant way of life and the booklet offers two examples of republican opposition to parades in Pomeroy and the Ormeau Road as illustrating that the exclusion of parades is a form of cultural apartheid. The authors claim that the Orange Order do not oppose rerouting for the sake of it, citing the example of several mini-twelfths that they have voluntarily rerouted so as not to cause offence. The concept of parity of esteem is mentioned, but the authors state that their preferred term is 'civil and religious liberty for all'.

The situation at Drumcree in 1995 is discussed, as is the symbolic significance of Drumcree to the Orange Order, with the prevailing belief that republicans were tampering with Protestant religious worship with the backing of the government of the Republic of Ireland. Montgomery and Witton believe that the Orange protest at Drumcree was a sign of frustration amongst a community which feels itself being disenfranchised. They suggest that the 'siege' greatly influenced other decisions on policing, given that after standing their ground, parades were subsequently allowed down the Lower Ormeau area and also along the walls of Derry Londonderry.

The authors conclude that the Orange Order does not intend to offend, but may do so inadvertently, and insist that they welcome negotiations with what they deem to be proper community groups, and not those which it believes are controlled by Sinn Féin. Significantly, it is proposed that the Order will give appropriate consideration to flags and types of bands in sensitive areas, and to stopping music or hymns near Catholic churches. More sensitivity is said to be required with respect to the use of the name UVF, which the Order argues in the past did have significance to the Protestant community, and it is made explicit that the Orange Order demands that Brethren behaviour on parade be beyond reproach.

60. Northern Ireland Affairs Committee (2004) *The Parades Commission and Public Processions (Northern Ireland) Act 1998.* London, The Stationery Office.

This report documents the Committee's response to the Quigley report of 2002 and raises concerns that the Quigley recommendations are out of date given the relatively quiet marching seasons of 2003-2004, which they suggest are evidence that disputes can be resolved through non-violence. The report is critical of the government's excessive consultation period of two years in its response to Quigley, and contends that the Parades Commission has made steady progress since its inception. The Committee are sceptical of Quigley's recommendations to replace the Commission with a new arrangement, believing that any change to the current arrangement could place the peace process at risk. The report suggests ways of improving the Parades Commission rather than replacing it.

The report outlines specific ways in which the Parades Commission could improve such as by making objections to parades clearer and more accessible, and by providing detailed feedback to organisers in good time. They also argue for fuller explanations in its determinations and greater detail about the potential impact of a parade, and suggest that the

Parades Commission review and strengthen its involvement in mediation and increase the number of Authorised Officers.

The Committee states that Quigley's assertion that responsibility for parades restrictions on public order grounds should rest with the police is unhelpful, as this puts the police in an impossible position. The police need to be seen to be neutral. It is proposed that the Parades Commission should seek to improve its organisational transparency, move forward in promoting mediation work, and redouble its efforts to secure the cooperation of the Orange Order.

The document defines the Parades Commission's functions under the Public Processions (Northern Ireland) Act of 1998 and details the requirements of notice for a parade. In particular, the Committee note that the Parades Commission has no powers in relation to protest meetings; these powers lie with the police. They argue against Quigley's proposal to make the police responsible for decision making in this case, as the police must be seen to be neutral, and the publication provides submissions from the Committee on the Administration of Justice (CAJ) and Democratic Dialogue to support this view. The Committee proceed to assess the Parades Commission's decision-making process and its guidelines, and argue that the Commission need to be more successful in promoting understanding of parades amongst the general public.

The report discusses human rights and expresses disquiet at Quigley's recommendation to incorporate Article 11 of the European Convention on Human Rights into the 1998 Public Order Act. The report also outlines deep concerns about Quigley's recommendation to divide responsibility for determining restrictions between two bodies, as this would create unnecessary legal confusion.

The report states that the Commission needs to clarify its position vis-à-vis parade followers, as at present the Commission claim they are not responsible for the followers, only the parade itself. The Committee suggest that transparency of the process should be a key concern for the Parades Commission. It is argued that the Commission needs to clearly distinguish the functions of mediation and determination, and that the consistency and standard of Authorised Officers needs to be improved. There are also concerns that mediation is seen as a box ticking exercise by some, so that their interests may be treated more favourably.

The report also expresses reservations about Quigley's recommendation of notification of parades to take place before 1st October every year, or no less than six months prior to a parade, and recommend keeping the existing 28-day period. The report recommends that marching bands should be registered as a priority under Section 12 of the 1998 Public Order Act.

The document concludes that the fact that the number of contentious parades has decreased while the number of parades taking place has increased shows the progress that the Parades Commission has made. In particular, the Parades Commission need to increase levels of confidence in it within the unionist community, explain the public order consideration, revitalise their role in mediation, and increase their operational transparency. The report sees great potential benefits in having one single body examine all relevant considerations, and recommends that the Commission keep all guidelines under review to improve their procedure.

61. Northern Ireland Forum for Political Dialogue: Standing Committee A (1997) *Review of the Parades Issue in Northern Ireland: Volume 1*. Belfast, Northern Ireland Forum for Political Dialogue.

This report aims to understand how parades are viewed by both sides of the community and is based on written submissions and oral evidence, primarily from within the unionist community. It aims to ascertain if the nature, frequency and routing of parades is likely to have contributed to protests against parades. The report also attempts to establish why protests against parades have increased over recent years, to assess the role of mediation in the disputes, and to examine the RUC's role and the difficulties they face in policing parades.

All of the contributors to the report accept the fundamental right to parade, although some suggested that with this right comes the responsibility to act sensitively. The study documents that the organisers of parades consider that the authorities have chosen to take action against legal parades rather than what they perceive to be illegal opposition, and believe this is directly linked to the Public Order (Northern Ireland) Order of 1987, and specifically Article 4 which can lead to restrictions on a parade if there is a threat of public disorder. Concerns by many respondents to the report around Article 7 of the 1987 Public Order Act led the authors to note that it was often termed a 'Lawbreakers Charter' by many who were in support of the right to parade.

The report states that current public order legislation is inadequate and provides incentives to those who threaten disorder in opposition to parades. The report claims that while nationalists do not understand the need for parading, unionists do not understand the reaction of nationalists to Loyal Order parades, as unionists themselves see parades as symbolic of the need to defend civil and religious liberty. The report also notes that contrary to some beliefs among unionists, many nationalists had only 'grudgingly tolerated' parades in the past.

The increase in contentious parades since the 1994 ceasefires is attributed to the role of Sinn Féin and the IRA in exploiting the issue and manipulating nationalist residents' groups for their own political ends, and the report is critical of the North report for making no mention of the role of Sinn Féin and the IRA in creating disorder. The Committee believe that the principle of consent is counterproductive and is contrary to the right of free expression and peaceful assembly.

The report contends that decisions taken on certain parades have resulted in the relationship between the RUC and unionist/loyalist community deteriorating, while some contributors believed that the decision to stop or reroute certain parades was a political one taken to appease the government of the Republic of Ireland.

The Committee concludes that the final decision regarding parades must remain with the RUC, and the Committee do not agree with the establishment of the Parades Commission, which they believe cannot be both a mediator and an adjudicator at the same time. The report makes several recommendations, which include the establishment of a code of practice to be adopted for both those involved in parades and in protest, that traditional parades should be protected under public order legislation and that the RUC enforce Article 7 of the 1987 Public Order (Northern Ireland) Order.

62. **Northern Ireland Forum for Political Dialogue: Standing Committee A** (1997) *Review of the Parades Issue in Northern Ireland: Volume 2.* **Belfast, Northern Ireland Forum for Political Dialogue.**

This large volume contains a collection of minutes of evidence on public order issues submitted to Standing Committee A of the Northern Ireland Forum for Political Dialogue in June 1997 by various individuals and organisations including the Community Relations Council, the Loyal

Orders, the Mediation Network of Northern Ireland, Ian Paisley, David Trimble and Robert McCartney.

63. Northern Ireland Office Steering Group, Second Report (2001) *Patten Report Recommendations 69 and 70 Relating to Public Order Equipment: A Research Programme into Alternative Policing Approaches Towards the Management of Conflict.* Belfast, Northern Ireland Office.

This is the second report of a Steering Group consisting of representatives of the Association of Chief Police Officers in England and Wales and the Home Office Police Scientific Development Branch. The report covers analysis and developments over a six-month period from the beginning of April to the end of October 2001, and aims to establish whether a less potentially lethal alternative to the baton round is available for public order situations. The report also seeks to review the public order equipment which is presently available or which could be developed in order to expand the range of tactical options available to operational commanders.

Chapter Two *The Management of Conflict* looks at the demands on the police in managing conflict in the community and provides an overview of policing disorder in the community. The section discusses the tactics available to the security forces and suggests they are dependent on the circumstances. Serious disorder requires a proper command structure, well thought-through strategy, large police numbers, protective equipment and the effective use of resources. The chapter provides a model of conflict management illustrating the various stages of decision-making used by police when dealing with disorder.

Public disorder in England and Wales is examined, notably in Oldham, Burnley and Leeds/Bradford, and the police response to such disturbances is documented. The chapter briefly deals with disorder in Northern Ireland in 2001, with recognition that rioters seemed aware of the police rules of engagement, in that many rioters approached shield walls with the belief that officers could not fire baton rounds at such a close proximity. The Steering Group notes several differences with respect to public disorder in Northern Ireland when compared with England and Wales, including a more organised nature, the role of paramilitary groups, an understanding of police tactics and the use of firearms and acid bombs by rioters.

Questionnaire responses and interviews with over fifty police officers note a significant difference between the experience of officers from Northern Ireland and those in Great Britain forces. The responses revealed difficulties in ascertaining 'safe' distance on the ground from which it would be possible to discharge a baton round, with widely differing perceptions on the intensity of threat in a given situation. The report considers the ability to create and maintain distance at an early stage of the disorder to be essential. Baton rounds are intended for use against targeted individuals as opposed to the crowd in general, and are only to be used as a pre-emptive measure at a distance greater than twenty metres away from the target.

Chapter Three *The Human Rights, Legal and Accountability Context* documents the United Nations basic principles on the use of force and firearms by law enforcement officials adopted by the eighth United Nations Congress in 1990. The section also highlights the UN Code of Conduct for Law Enforcement Officials of 1979 and the relevant articles of the European Convention on Human Rights. The research also addresses domestic criminal and common law, particularly section 3 of the Criminal Law Act (Northern Ireland) 1967, and Article 88 of the Police and Criminal Evidence (Northern Ireland) Order 1989. It is suggested that the police have generally relied upon the provisions of section 3 of the 1967 Act as both the legal authority and the benchmark against which any use of force will be judged. It and PACE both require that any force used is 'reasonable in the circumstances'. The test for using both lethal and potentially lethal force is that it is absolutely necessary, and proportionality is identified as the key factor in the use of force.

The section also notes other legislation that has a bearing on the policing situation and provides significant detail on the Police (Northern Ireland) Act 2000, while Klenig's work is stated to have an importance with regards to the use of force. He identified five factors that are relevant to the ethical assessment of the use of intermediate and indeed deadly force. These include intentions, seemliness, proportionality, minimisation and practicability. The chapter also outlines the Secretary of State's role under Section 53 of the Police Act 2000, and identifies the Northern Ireland Human Rights Commission's report on RUC fired baton rounds between 1997 and 2000 as containing a number of criticisms and recommendations leading to a police review of their reporting format.

Chapter Four *Acceptability* notes that the Human Rights Audit Framework is used as a set of criteria against which any proposal or equipment could be evaluated. The Framework also addresses strategic, ethical, operational and societal considerations.

Chapter Five *Use of Baton Rounds and Other Equipment* provides an account of the usage of plastic baton rounds in Northern Ireland for every year between 1981 and October 2001. The years in which there was the highest number of baton round discharges were 1981 and 1996, and after 1999 there was a huge drop in the use of baton rounds since the introduction of new guidelines from 1 August 1999. This led in June 2001 to the introduction of the L21A1 round, and an independent medical committee found that the new baton round was more consistently accurate and had a reduced probability of being life threatening.

Chapter Six *The Review of Less Lethal Technologies Undertaken by the Police Scientific Development Branch* outlines the testing process for a number of devices including impact devices or kinetic energy rounds, long range chemical delivery devices, water cannons and electrical devices such as tasers and disorientation devices. The chapter discusses water cannon in detail and notes that they have been used in Northern Ireland since the early 1970s, but suggests that problems linked to water cannon include poor manoeuvrability, inadequate protection, lack of access to water supplies and their small capacity. The report claims that jets of water at high pressure can also be capable of inflicting serious injury, such as bone fractures.

Chapter Seven *Medical Assessment* provides an overview of some of the potential medical issues associated with the use of certain less lethal weapon technologies. In assessing the potential for injury, the report suggests that it is necessary to consider both the accuracy and consistency of the projectile with other factors including the quality of the training received by the user of the weapon. The Steering Group are of the view that water cannon are inherently inaccurate, with the most damage likely to be done to an individual's eye. The report recommends more immediate in-depth research into the use of water cannon.

The Steering Group conclude that alternative equipment to baton rounds or 'less' lethal weapons cannot be placed in a single hierarchical continuum of force, and the group note that the risk involved in alternative systems to a large degree still depends on the skill and training of the user.

64. Northern Ireland Office Steering Group Third Report (2002) *Patten Report Recommendations 69 and 70 Relating to Public Order Equipment: A Research Programme into Alternative Policing Approaches Towards The Management Of Conflict.* **Belfast, Northern Ireland Office.**

The report aims to establish whether a less potentially lethal alternative to the baton round is available, and to review the public order equipment which is presently available or could be developed in order to expand the range of tactical options available to operational commanders. The Steering Group argue that in terms of the use of force, a strict legal test is not enough, and that issues of morality and ethics are also significant, as are personal, international and community perceptions. They highlight the importance of strategic and local partnerships, and criticise the fact that a safe and effective alternative to the current baton round, the L21A1, has not yet been identified despite two million pounds being spent on development and research since the last report.

It is asserted that managing conflict is not just about technological issues, but also policing with the community, conflict resolution and community safety, and it is further suggested that it is important to develop public order policing with community policing to reduce the negative impact should the former have to be resorted to. The report sees community policing and policing disorder as inextricably linked, and examines what it outlines are the most important aspects of community policing: service delivery, partnership, problem solving, accountability and empowerment.

The Steering Group provides illustrative examples of Public Disorder in Northern Ireland and overseas, and states that the police have had to deal with serious public disorder in 2002 in the Ardoyne area and Drumcree in particular. The report documents the difficulties the PSNI faced during January 2002 in North Belfast, with forty eight police officers injured and four civilians receiving gunshot wounds from rioters or paramilitaries. The report argues that this demonstrates how a spontaneous outbreak of violence can lead to severe and sustained rioting.

The publication contains a summary of the main points emerging from the International Law Enforcement Forum, which took place in October 2002. One issue emerging was that large-scale public disorder in North America tended to involve people coming into a neighbourhood with the intent to cause trouble. This differed from the regular pattern in Northern Ireland where the police role is often to ensure that opposing crowds are kept apart, frequently at the interface between the streets in which they live. The participants felt that the UK's formalised process of Gold, Silver and Bronze command structures promoted less lethal weapon usage in pre-planned or protracted situations.

The Steering Group proceed to outline the guidelines on the use of baton rounds by the Armed Forces in Northern Ireland in terms of the rules of engagement. These state that:

- Baton rounds are only to be used at the command of the designated local commander, only when there is no alternative and only if the user is fully trained.
- Warning is to be given verbally beforehand, and where possible a visible demonstration of intent is given.
- Baton rounds are to be fired at selected individuals, not indiscriminately, and should be aimed at the lower part of the body and not be fired at less than twenty metres distance unless there is an immediate threat to loss of life.

The report makes recommendations for the policing of public order situations, including that video cameras are to be used, soldiers are to be interviewed soon after use, and that guidelines should be developed in tandem between the police and army for the use of baton rounds.

Also available: Northern Ireland Office Steering Group First Report (2001) *Patten Report Recommendations 69 and 70 Relating to Public Order Equipment: A Research Programme into Alternative Policing Approaches Towards The Management Of Conflict.* Belfast, Northern Ireland Office.

65. Northern Ireland Policing Board (2005) *Human Rights: Monitoring the Compliance of the Police Service of Northern Ireland with the Human Rights Act 1998. Annual Report 2005.* Belfast, Northern Ireland Policing Board.

This publication states that those who want to parade have recognised human rights including the right to freedom of expression and freedom of assembly. They also have the right to expect the police to protect their exercise of these rights so long as they themselves remain peaceful. Equally, others who do not want parades which they consider to be offensive to pass through the area in which they live also have recognised human rights. These include the right to protest and the right to peaceful enjoyment of their home environment.

The report documents the requirements of the Human Rights Act of 1998, particularly Article 8 (the right to respect for private and family life and to a home), and Articles 9, 10, and 11 (freedom of religion, expression and assembly respectively), which taken together provide a right of protest. These articles are not absolute, and can be restricted as long as any restriction is lawful, necessary and proportionate. The report sets out that the mere fact that a protest, march or procession may annoy others or even offend them is not a sufficient basis for restricting it.

The Policing Board note that the Parades Commission's guidelines require it to have due regard to any public disorder or damage to property which may result from the procession, any disruption to the life of the community that the procession may cause, any impact the procession may have on relationships within the community, any failure to comply with the Code of Conduct and the desirability of allowing a procession customarily held along a particular route. The Parades Commission therefore has the primary responsibility for ensuring that an appropriate balance is achieved between those wishing to parade, those opposed and those who live in the vicinity of those parades. Protest meetings are dealt with differently, with notice going to the police. The Police Service of Northern Ireland's responsibility is to police any determination of the Commission and to take appropriate operational decisions to that end within the framework of the applicable law.

The report briefly discusses the PSNI's Public Order Policy, whose purpose is to outline policy in relation to public events including public processions in compliance with the principles of the Human Rights Act and other international human rights instruments. The report recommends that the Policy be amended to include: a summary of the relevant provisions of the European Convention on Human Rights; a commentary on the application of these provisions in the public order context and some guidance on factors likely to be relevant in balancing human rights in the public order context.

The Report also addresses the PSNI's Protest Activity Policy, which states that protest activity in a democratic society is a legitimate means of expressing views and opinions, and that protestors and counter-protestors have a fundamental right to peaceful assembly and to demonstrate without fear of physical violence from those who oppose their ideas. The document recommends that the PSNI review its General Order on the Public Processions (Northern Ireland) Act 1998 and relationship with the Parades Commission. All officers should be required to know and understand the basis upon which the Parades Commission issues its determinations and the agreed protocols for communication between the PSNI and the Parades Commission. The report recommends that the PSNI should review its arrangements with the Parades Commission and agree protocols for effective communication between itself and the Parades Commission as a priority. The report also stresses that the PSNI needs to set out its relationship with the military and then agree liaison procedures for joint operations.

The Ardoyne parade of 12 July 2004 is examined and it is claimed that at all stages those responsible for policing the parade considered that the determinations of the Parades Commission applied to followers or supporters of the parades and planned the operation on that basis. The decision of Mr. Justice Weatherup on 9 July 2004 had a profound effect on the policing operation, as from then on the PSNI could not lawfully rely on the determinations of the Parades Commission as a basis for preventing followers or supporters of the parades from proceeding through the contentious part of the route. After this decision, the PSNI only had power to prevent the followers proceeding along that part of the route if they presented a threat to the peace. Since there was no evidence that the parade followers' behaviour on 12 July went beyond that of a following, the PSNI had no power to prevent them from proceeding along the contentious part of the route and the PSNI did not breach the Parades Commission's determinations. The report identifies some serious concerns, principally that the interpretation by the Parades Commission and the judgment of Mr. Justice Weatherup excluding those who follow the parade will have a profound and detrimental effect on the ability of the PSNI to police parades in the future. It is contended that this goes to the heart of the legal framework of Northern Ireland, and in this respect better communication between the PSNI and the Parades Commission is needed.

Concerns were raised about PSNI follow-through after the annual Public Order Debrief which takes place at the end of the marching season. It is recommended that the PSNI should assign responsibility internally for reviewing the annual Public Order Debrief Reports, for liasing with the relevant departments within the PSNI who are responsible for considering or investigating particular problems identified and for overseeing any changes proposed as a result of this exercise. The PSNI should also conduct an internal after-the-event audit of a random selection of public order operations as part of its annual debrief process, and in particular the PSNI should include consideration of community responses and parade organisers' and participants' views on the policing of parades over the marching season as part of its annual debrief process.

66. Northern Ireland Policing Board (2005) *Monitoring the Compliance of the Police Service of Northern Ireland with the Human Rights Act 1998: Report on the Policing of the Ardoyne Parades 12th July 2005, and the Whiterock Parade 10th September 2005.* **Belfast, Northern Ireland Policing Board.**

This report documents the policing operations which took place at the Ardoyne Parades on 12 July 2005 and the Whiterock Parade of 10 September 2005, and aims to ascertain whether or not the PSNI complied with the terms of the Human Rights Act of 1998. The report notes the determinations made by the Parades Commission with respect to the Ardoyne and Whiterock events, and describes the events as they unfolded on the ground. The Policing Board note that during the Ardoyne parade there were at least nine blast bombs thrown, one hundred and five police officers and eight members of the public were injured. The police fired Attenuating Energy Projectiles (AEPs) striking nine individuals. At Whiterock, one hundred and fifty live rounds were fired at the police and military, plus hundreds of blast and petrol bombs thrown. Ninety three police officers were injured. In response, the PSNI discharged six live rounds, two hundred and thirty eight AEP rounds and deployed water cannon.

The report considers that on this occasion, policing in Ardoyne was careful and considered and both those on parade and those engaged in protest had their human rights upheld. The report refutes allegations that the deployment of water cannon occurred too early in the operation and is also satisfied that the police complied with the 1998 Human Rights Act with regards to the discharge of AEPs. However, the report states that the lack of visible identification numbers on police officers is unsatisfactory. The report documents a number of recommendations arising from the policing of the Ardoyne parade, which include a need for human rights advisers to be available to the police at all stages, a need to obtain modern screening equipment and a need for police identification markings to be clearly visible.

In relation to the Whiterock parade the Policing Board suggest that the strategic, tactical and operational planning of the police operation was careful and considered, particularly given the lives rounds fired at police. It is highlighted that while the police fired six live rounds in response, and deployed water cannon, the Policing Board contend that they did not see or hear anything which was in breach of the Human Rights Act, but they recommended that the PSNI review its procedures relating to its consultations with the interested parties. The police complied with the

AEP Impact Rounds Policy and also the Human Rights Act, and their use of live fire and AEPs is argued to have been proportionate and in compliance with the Human Rights Act. The Policing Board note two specific concerns regarding police behaviour, including that police officers allegedly beat an individual on the legs and that another individual was struck and kicked by police officers. The report suggests that the PSNI should consider making some of the video footage publicly available.

67. Northern Ireland Policing Board (2006) *Monitoring the Compliance of the Police Service of Northern Ireland with the Human Rights Act 1998. Human Rights: Annual Report 2006.* Belfast, Northern Ireland Policing Board.

This report considers whether the policing of parades complies with the requirements of the Human Rights Act, whether the Police Service of Northern Ireland properly polices Parades Commission decisions and whether any use of force by the PSNI is justified.

Chapter Seven *Public Order* highlights that the statutory framework regulating parades and protests changed on 14th May 2005 when the Public Processions (Amendment) (Northern Ireland) Order 2005 came into force. The Policing Board state that one of the key problems identified in the Ardoyne parades report of 2004 was that the Parades Commission had no power to issue determinations imposing conditions on those supporting or following parades. The 2005 Order removed that difficulty and the Parades Commission now has the power to impose conditions on any persons supporting a parade, as well as having the power to impose conditions on protest meetings.

The report documents that the Policing Board were involved in the monitoring of parades in 2006, particularly the Tour of the North and Whiterock parades, both of which passed off without violence. In relation to the Tour of the North it was noted that an agreed small protest at the shop fronts led to a significantly reduced policing presence of only six neighbourhood police officers. The Whiterock parade, despite local tensions, also passed off without incident. For the Twelfth of July parade along Crumlin Road, the Policing Board note in the evening a small number of missiles were thrown at the parade.

The report concludes that the strategic, tactical and operational planning of the policing operations was careful and considered and that the human rights of all individuals had been taken into account at all stages. The Board believe that policing was effective and carried out with a high degree of flexibility and sensitivity. They report on an impressive level of consultation, planning and integrated decision-making across districts, particularly during the Whiterock parade, by the North and West Belfast District Command Unit commanders.

It is argued that the success which prevented major violence was principally due to two factors, firstly the dialogue and negotiation between parade and protest organisers' in advance which led to two instances of agreement and secondly the extensive community consultation carried out by senior PSNI commanders throughout the planning process. This either ensured a sensitive police response in support of community arrangements or, if agreement was not reached, provided a flexible, proportionate and transparent policing response. The Policing Board welcome dialogue between parade and protest organisers and also commend the extensive community consultation undertaken by senior PSNI commanders as highlighting their flexibility. These factors are said to have made a significant impact on the very different nature of parades in 2006.

68. North, Peter (1997) *Independent Review of Parades and Marches.* Belfast, The Stationery Office.

This report was commissioned in response to violence at the Drumcree church parade in the summer of 1996. It examines the background to the parading organisations in Northern Ireland, and summarises the events of the summer of 1996 and the subsequent riots believed to have cost ten million pounds in police funds, and over twenty million pounds cost of criminal damage.

The views and concerns of Loyal Order representatives and nationalist residents' groups are examined, which the report believes essentially highlights the dichotomy between the unionist position of civil and religious liberty in allowing parades versus the concept of parity of esteem and rights of locals espoused traditionally by nationalists. Demographic change is seen as a key factor in making the unionist community feel less secure and therefore more defensive in relation to any perceived threat to their parades. Many unionists interviewed believed that the republican movement, having failed to defeat unionists by violence, decided to take politics onto the streets and exploit the 1987 Public Order (Northern Ireland) Order. North suggests that the Royal

Ulster Constabulary's role in decisions regarding parades and also their subsequent enforcement damaged their reputation in both communities, and the report argues for a need for local accommodation to parade disputes.

The report discusses the policing of public order and the policing of the events of 1996. It is contended that there needs to be improved strategic thinking and contingency planning by the RUC and Northern Ireland Office among others, with an emphasis needed on greater understanding from both sides, and a focus on achieving local discussions and accommodation. North believes that it is not right or fair that the RUC are required to make and enforce a decision concerning a parade, and suggests that the present law needs to be changed as it is presently an incentive for disorder.

The fundamental principles of the North Report include the ability to protect the right to peaceful assembly subject to certain qualifications: responsibility, local accommodation, that legislation must not provide encouragement to promote disorder and that procedures should be proportional. The study specifically criticises the Public Order (Northern Ireland) Order 1987 as it fails to recognise the rights of both peaceful assembly and the rights of those living in an area where the parade passes. There is a need for statutory criteria which take clearer account of underlying rights and responsibilities of all those concerned, and for a determination by someone other than the police as to whether conditions are required to be imposed in relation to contentious parades if agreement is not reached locally. North subsequently considers the arguments for and against an independent body, and concludes that the creation of a new body would allow interested parties to put their views forward about proposed parades, encourage them to settle differences locally and if that proved impossible, to come to a view itself on what, if any, conditions should be imposed.

The report's main recommendations include:

- Responsibility for reaching conclusions regarding disputed parades should be with the Parades Commission and not the RUC.
- If the Chief Constable is sufficiently concerned about a determination, he may inform the Secretary of State, who may reconsider the Commission's decision. North recommends that in the extreme circumstances of the determination of the Commission being defied, the police should retain the power to intervene on public order grounds.

- A new offence is recommended to penalise individuals who, through force of numbers or threat of disorder, contravene the legal determinations of the Commission.

The proposed Parades Commission's guidelines should take into consideration factors including the route, the impact on the local community, the purpose of the parade, the main features of the parade and the approach of the interested parties relating to past behaviour, tradition and the numbers taking part in the parade. A Code of Conduct should cover accountability, stewarding, behaviour and displays of both participants of a parade and protestors. It is argued that the alcohol laws relating to Great Britain should be extended to Northern Ireland, and that government in consultation with the relevant authorities should consider introducing a band registration scheme.

The report states that the right to freedom of assembly is subject to certain qualifications, but includes a responsibility to act sensitively and with respect to the possible effects on relationships within the community. The proposed newly created Parades Commission should therefore have the power to impose conditions on a contentious parade and any restrictions on disputed parades should be imposed by the Commission, and not the RUC.

69. Orr, Sir John (2005) *Review of Marches and Parades in Scotland.* Edinburgh, Scottish Executive.

This report looks at types of procession in Scotland, the current legislative position and how local authorities currently take decisions on parades. The review also discusses the situation in Scotland in comparison with England and Northern Ireland.

The power to prohibit processions or impose restrictions on parades in Scotland rests with the Local Authorities. Orr sets out the legislative framework within which decisions are taken, and looks at human rights legislation and particularly Article 11 of the European Conventions. The Civic Government (Scotland) Act 1982 requires seven days notice before a parade and is the statutory framework for holding public processions in Scotland. The publication discusses current processes for taking decisions about marches, and argues for a greater degree of consistency in approaches, as processions 'commonly or customarily' held are not subject to notification, although local authorities can still impose conditions them. A number of local authorities have developed very straightforward guidance for those organising processions, with very few complaints made in Scotland regarding parades, while those which are made often relate more to noise, litter and disruption, and less to sectarian behaviour. The report notes that the number of notified processions is increasing, with a nine percent increase between 2001-2003, and Orange parades have seen the steadiest growth, rising from 800 in 2001 to 853 in 2003.

Orr contrasts the situation in Northern Ireland with England and Scotland, highlighting good practice in London and Merseyside, whereby there is a planning process involving organisations involved in marches who sign a 'statement of intent'. The report suggests that in England the guidance notes provided by the police to the parade organisers and planning meetings at the initial stages lead to more effective planning, which leads to greater consistency in approaches to marches overall. The good working relationship in Liverpool between the Orange Order and the police, which involves early discussions and an operational planning handbook, allows for more effective stewarding and again a more consistent approach.

The report makes thirty eight recommendations for the Scottish Executive, including a call for an increase in the notification period to twenty eight days to allow the local authorities to deliberate in more detail and communicate their determinations to organisers. Orr recommends the need for a single gateway between the local authorities and the police, and that there needs to be better coordination between the organisations. He also recommends that there needs to be effective monitoring arrangements through the Scottish Executive to make sure that local authorities and the police are implementing new procedures. Orr suggests the current approach could be improved by implementing a code of conduct, providing guidelines on the decision making process, holding a debriefing after the event, increased communication with communities, and more effective monitoring. Any decisions taken should also be more fully explained to the organisations involved.

In terms of informing and involving the community, the report suggests that local authorities should prepare an annual digest of processions with organisers at the beginning of the calendar year, with up to date information on forthcoming processions. It is argued that there is a need for a mechanism to enable the community and others to express views and to be taken into account. It is also contended in this respect that local authorities should remain responsible for decisions in order to retain an important link which communities can use to influence decisions which impact upon them.

The report recommends a written, signed notification with the key procession information to be implemented for organisers of processions. This should be followed by a meeting facilitated by the local authority, police and organisers and should result in a signed outcome, with a 'permit to process' issued after notification had been agreed. A Code of Conduct should also be set out within this 'Permit to Process', and local authorities should produce a 'How To' guide for organisers. The report raises concerns about the lack of available statistics on parades, and calls for police and local authorities to keep statistics on the numbers of processions and costs. The report concludes that there is a need for stricter control on the behaviour of bands and their followers, and that there is a perceived need to tackle problems associated with alcohol consumption at parades through civic codes.

70. Parades Commission (2005) *Public Processions and Related Protest Meetings: Guidelines, A Code of Conduct and Procedural Rules.* Belfast, Parades Commission.

The Parades Commission's *Guidelines* are based on the premise that the rights of peaceful assembly and freedom of expression under the European Convention of Human Rights are important rights to be enjoyed by all, although these rights are not absolute. The Guidelines are designed as a means of testing the validity of counter arguments to the right to freedom of assembly and of expression. Section 8 (1) of the Public Processions (Northern Ireland) Act 1998 empowers the Commission to impose conditions on public processions, while Section 9a of the Act allows the Commission to impose conditions on protest meetings. In terms of public processions the legislation requires that the Parades Commission have due regard to:

- The Guidelines.
- Any public disorder or damage to property which may result from the procession.
- Any disruption to the life of the community which may occur.
- Any impact on relationships within the community.
- Failure to comply with the Code of Conduct.
- The desirability of allowing customarily held parades.

For protest meetings, the Commission are also required to have due regard to:

- Restriction of freedom of movement by locals.

- Restriction of commercial activity.
- Restriction of access to public amenities such as hospitals.
- Restriction of access to places of worship.
- Duration of procession or protest.

In terms of any possible impact on relationships which a public procession may have, the Commission must take into account the extent to which the area is mainly residential or commercial, the demographic balance within the area, the presence of churches or sensitive sites and the purpose of the public procession, as well as the desirability of allowing a parade on a customarily held route.

The Parades Commission's *Code of Conduct* is a source of advice for those organising public processions and marches for any purpose in public places, and for those organising related protest meetings. Compliance with the Code of Conduct is a factor which the Parades Commission takes into account in deciding whether or not to impose conditions on a parade or public procession.

The Parades Commission's *Procedural Rules* explain how the Parades Commission will gather information which may inform the exercise of its statutory functions, including the views of supporters and opposers of public processions or protest meetings, and how they will issue determinations on individual public processions or related protest meetings. The Procedural Rules include requiring twenty eight days notification for processions and fourteen days for protests, acquiring information in the form of details of past processions, details, numbers, past conduct, demographic mix and the location of sensitive areas. They also include taking evidence in a confidential manner, supporting mediation at a local level, making formal determinations and reviewing any decisions or determinations.

71. **Parades Commission (2006)** *Parading in a Peaceful Northern Ireland: Forward View and Review of Procedures.* **Belfast, Parades Commission.**

This publication is essentially a review of the procedures of the Parades Commission and aims to provide an understanding of how the Commission operates, addressing the key issues raised by individuals and groups during the Review Process. The report documents a marked reduction in violence and disorder at parades in 2006, and notes that of all of the thousands of parades which take place annually, the Commission only looks closely at fewer than seven percent of them. The authors suggest a major reason for this quiet marching season has been the work of many people at the grassroots coupled with outreach work over ten months to create an environment where there is a greater understanding over parades issues. The Commission outline their firm commitment to dialogue between local people as the only way to reach a lasting solution on parades.

It is acknowledged that many in the Protestant community see parades as a demonstration of their religion, culture and sense of community, and that the right of assembly in principle needs to be upheld, although subject to proportionate limitation were necessary. The publication also acknowledges that for many nationalists, the Loyal Order parades are seen as triumphalist and anti-Catholic. Similarly, it is argued that residents' groups need to address perceptions held by some within the unionist community that they are orchestrated by Sinn Féin and working towards a wider political agenda to suppress Protestant culture. The Commission stress that there is no right of veto on a parade, and that while there is both a right to parade and to protest, neither is absolute. It is suggested that parade tensions can undermine political progress. The Commission argue for a more strategic and long-term position to be taken on parading and protest in Northern Ireland as at present the approach is too localised and specific regarding individual parades.

The paper describes the consultation process involved in the Review of Procedures and outlines opinions gathered, the Commission's response and recommendations of the Review Process. The Parades Commission make a number of recommendations including that if a parade is contentious the notification process should be longer than twenty eight days. The paper also recommends amending the review process and documents to make procedures clearer.

72. Pat Finucane Centre (1995) *One Day in August.* Derry Londonderry, Pat Finucane Centre.

This is a report into the allegations by the Bogside Residents' Group of human rights abuses arising out of the Apprentice Boys' parade in Derry Londonderry on 12 August 1995. The report is based on evidence from eyewitnesses and protestors, residents, businessmen, community workers and local city centre workers.

The Apprentice Boys last applied to walk the walls of Derry Londonderry in 1969 which led to the Battle of the Bogside and they have been denied permission ever since. The authors state that the right to parade must now be qualified to include satisfactory agreement concerning the marshalling and stewarding of the parade and behaviour of the Apprentice Boys. The key principle in the report is one of consent, and the Pat Finucane Centre say that no one has the right to parade where they are not wanted. They also suggest that a substantial number of the Apprentice Boys were involved in behaviour which was abusive, sectarian, sexist and often under the influence of alcohol. It is argued that Derry City Council has an important role to play, and the report recommends that a group within the council should meet as wide a range of organisations as possible with an interest in the issue with a view to facilitating an agreement which all sides can live with.

The reasons why people oppose parades are discussed and the report recognises that there is a belief in the loyalist community that Irish nationalists are deeply opposed to the Irish Protestant heritage. The Pat Finucane Centre argue that this is not the case, and that many Irish nationalists welcome the theatre and pageantry of the parades. It is suggested that opposition is related to the behaviour of a significant minority of the Apprentice Boys, particularly at Butchers Gate, and which included some members waving their sashes at nationalist protestors. The document notes the powerful symbolism of the image of men in bowler hats in sashes on top of the walls looking down over the Bogside. The report is critical of the apparent inability of the leadership of the organisation to do anything about sectarian behaviour. In the incidents that led to the rioting on the Saturday and Sunday nights, the report blames the RUC, and it is also contended that plastic bullets were shot from too close a range and at head height. There were more plastic bullets fired in one weekend in Derry Londonderry than at any comparable period in the last five years, and the report concludes that the RUC were the primary cause of the breakdown in community relations and resulting disorder in Derry Londonderry.

The Pat Finucane Centre recommend that the Apprentice Boys not be allowed to parade the wall without consent, and that they are only allowed to parade in the city centre following satisfactory agreement concerning the stewarding of the parade and the behaviour of the Apprentice Boys. It is also recommended that the political parties and the media should commit to facilitating good relations on the basis of toleration and respect, and in terms of policing the report calls for an immediate end to the use of plastic bullets and a resolution of what the Pat Finucane Centre see as a crisis in policing.

73. Pat Finucane Centre (1996) *In the Line of Fire: Derry, July 1996.* **Derry Londonderry, Pat Finucane Centre.**

This report focuses on the events in Derry Londonderry following the Drumcree standoff on 7 July 1996. The report was comprised using a compilation of news articles and interviews, with a stated purpose to highlight the abuse of human rights in Derry Londonderry. The report's main concern is with the way the Royal Ulster Constabulary initiated and responded to civil disturbances in Derry Londonderry and focuses on policing rather than on the parade itself. The Pat Finucane Centre state that parades have never been far from controversy, and the authors contend that the basis of opposition to parades is based on the concept of 'parity of esteem'.

The document asserts that the RUC is unacceptable as a police force, and questions the position of Sir Patrick Mayhew as Secretary of State. The publication suggests that the RUC broke their own guidelines and initiated a series of events leading to three nights of heavy rioting in Derry Londonderry. The report provides a chronology of events from 7-15 July. The publication highlights that over one hundred people were treated in hospital, and claims that the RUC instigated trouble by deliberately targeting young people coming out of pubs in the town. In discussing the varying types of injuries received by locals, the Pat Finucane Centre contend that people seeking treatment at Altnagelvin hospital were confronted by RUC officers and that the RUC had to be asked to leave by the hospital's Chief Executive. The report documents the events leading up to the death of Dermot McShane, who was crushed beneath an Army Saracen, and also notes that the riot damage in the city affected many locals adversely, with many losing income and many local family businesses being destroyed. The Pat Finucane Centre blames Ian Paisley and David Trimble for unleashing a wave of sectarianism through their actions at Drumcree.

The authors assert that the RUC were the main protagonists in the violence, and that there was an unlawful use of plastic bullets which resulted in injuries to many people. The report makes several recommendations including among others, a call for the RUC to be replaced and plastic bullets to be banned. The report concludes that the continued use of plastic bullets could be a serious blockage to a lasting peace settlement.

74. Pat Finucane Centre (1997) For God and Ulster: *An Alternative Guide to the Loyal Orders.* Derry Londonderry, Pat Finucane Centre.

This booklet proposes to offer an alternative guide to the Loyal Orders, attempting to offer a basic outline of the Loyal Orders' structure, history and development. The document states that it is an attempt to understand why so many people have a problem with the Loyal Orders. The booklet deals with the controversy surrounding contentious parades and the political role of the Loyal Orders both past and present, and provides a chronological history of parading disputes throughout the nineteenth century. The publication asserts that the Orders are indeed religious, cultural and social organisations that have a right to parade, but that their political involvement has often served to delay civil, religious and political liberties to others.

The history of the formation of the Orange Order and its membership is examined, as is its role as an organisation which aimed to create 'Protestant unity', linking Anglicans, Presbyterians and other denominations in one movement to become an increasingly effective political force. The report then moves on to discuss the Orange Order's political history, as well as documenting the Stormont years between 1921 and 1972. The Order is seen as being a political force within the strength of Unionism, with the ability to hold together a strategically focused power bloc, uniting the Protestant working classes and the unionist elite. The report recognises the social role that the Orange Order plays within the Protestant community, particularly in rural areas. These social and cultural functions, the report argues, are important in understanding why individuals join in the first place. It is suggested that there was a historical, social and political role also, and that the Protestant working classes were never allowed to have their anger drift from the traditional enemies of 'Rome'.

The authors proceed to discuss the relationship which they see between some elements within loyalist paramilitarism and the Loyal Orders. The Pat Finucane Centre recognises that the Orders never formally encouraged any loyalist paramilitary groups and the majority of members were opposed to sectarian attacks. However, they discuss links between loyalist paramilitaries and the Orange Order, and suggest that there is an ambiguous relationship between the bands and the Orange Order, and speaks of the double standards of some members of the Order who will not meet members of residents' groups with previous terrorist convictions, yet have met leading loyalist paramilitaries.

The relationship with law and order and the police is explored, and the Pat Finucane Centre alleges that Catholic officers in the RUC were deliberately excluded from serving during disturbances in Derry Londonderry in 1996. That same year, seven RUC officers were suspended for their involvement in Orange Order protests, and in 1996 two members of the Police Authority themselves were members of the Loyal Orders which the report believes shows a close relationship between the Loyal Orders and the RUC. The report concludes with a discussion of the events surrounding the disturbances at Drumcree in 1995.

75. PeaceWatch Ireland (1997) *Looking into the Abyss: Witnesses' Report from Garvaghy Road, Portadown. July 4th - July 6th 1997.* New York, PeaceWatch Ireland.

This publication provides a summary of events on the Garvaghy Road in 1997 and accuses the British security forces of 'unnecessary brutality'. Some pictures of scenes on the road between 4 and 6 July are also contained within the report. PeaceWatch Ireland documents findings of violence and brutality, although the publication does not provide any statistics for these findings. The findings include the belief that the British military chose a military rather than a political solution, that the British government pursued a military strategy resulting in civil and human rights violations, that the security forces fired plastic bullets in an unnecessary use of force and that badge numbers for identification purposes were not visible on half of security force members. PeaceWatch Ireland recommend a total ban on plastic bullets, the creation of a new police force, the establishment of the principle of consent for parades as they suggest the Parades Commission is inadequate and has no enforcement, and they also request that the media report the situation more accurately.

76. Police Ombudsman for Northern Ireland (2002) *Baton Rounds Report 2002.* Belfast, Police Ombudsman for Northern Ireland.

This is the first of two publications summarising seven reports by the Police Ombudsman of Northern Ireland on the discharge of baton rounds in 2001 and 2002. The report documents seven incidents: three each in Ardoyne and Portadown and one in Lurgan which involved the firing of thirty six baton rounds, which struck twenty six people. In total, one hundred and seventeen police officers were injured in the disturbances. The report states that the deployment of rounds was in full accordance with Association of Chief Police Officers guidelines and that all the incidents had involved attacks on the police using bricks, masonry, fireworks, petrol, paint, acid and blast bombs.

77. Police Ombudsman for Northern Ireland (2005) *Baton Rounds Report 2005*. Belfast, Police Ombudsman for Northern Ireland.

This is a summary of twenty four reports by the Police Ombudsman for Northern Ireland to the Secretary of State, Northern Ireland Policing Board and the Chief Constable on the discharge of baton rounds by police during 2001 and 2002. This publication notes there were two hundred and ninety nine baton rounds discharged in twenty four incidents, the majority in North and East Belfast. The report finds that in all incidents the use of baton rounds was justified and in accordance with regulations.

The guidance and legislation covering the use of baton rounds is examined, and the report then discusses in detail each incident, providing conclusions and recommendations for the police. The report provides an overview of accuracy, the physical area struck, the status of the victim and the range that the person involved was away from baton gunners. The report documents that nineteen of the twenty four incidents were in full accordance with the guidelines. The Ombudsman's Office also identify some difficulties associated with the police delay in contacting the office, a lack of baton gun assistants, a lack of full video evidence, overworked baton gunners and the presence of semi-automatic weapons in riot situations. It is contended that there was a frequent lack of proper video evidence of baton round discharges, and it is recommended that the police should deploy evidence gatherers alongside baton gunners.

78. Purdie, Bob (1990) *Politics in the Streets: The Origins of the Civil Rights Movement in Northern Ireland*. Belfast, Blackstaff Press.

This book discusses the origins of the civil rights movement in Northern Ireland of the late 1960s, and argues that the civil rights movement was innovative as it restricted itself to demanding legal and constitutional rights within the UK. Purdie claims that the mass demonstration in Newry after Bloody Sunday in 1972 was the movement's last great civil rights march and also the movement's funeral procession.

Chapter One *The O'Neill Years, 1962-1968* examines some of the attempts at modernisation and reform attempted during the years of Captain Terence O'Neill from March 1963 onwards. This era saw attempts to improve community relations, highlighted by the talks between the Orange Order and the Ancient Order of Hibernians in 1963, and the author suggests that this period also saw the ecumenical movement standing up to the Orange Order. The section outlines that uncertainty and the divisions among the Orange Order were apparent during the O'Neill years, and that the Order's indecisive leadership failed to prevent the growth of a strong, extreme, minority loyalist opposition. The chapter states that the emergence of the civil rights movement enabled Ian Paisley to move to the centre stage and play on the fears many unionists had of the movement as a front for republicanism. By 1968, it is suggested that O'Neill had also succeeded in alienating most Catholics as well, and Purdie notes that an important part of the process was that Catholic and liberal Protestant opposition to the government took to the streets as they had exhausted all other effective means to bring about change.

Chapter Two *The New Opposition* discusses the background to the formation of the Nationalist Party, and suggests that by 1965 the opposition to the unionist regime were making real progress challenging by parliamentary means. Purdie notes that Labour after 1949 became largely Belfast and Protestant based and that Orangeism was not incompatible with Labour voting. Several candidates of the Northern Ireland Labour Party in this period, including Cecil Allen, refer to the problems associated with unionist flute bands, and by 1966 although Labour had failed to establish itself in Northern Ireland, it was one more factor in a process that was forcing opposition onto the streets.

The role of the Ulster Liberal Party and its chairman the Reverend Albert McElroy is assessed, and it is documented that McElroy defended the right of republicans to hold commemorations of the 1916 Rising, appearing on platforms with republicans and nationalists to appeal against the ban on republican clubs. McElroy called for O'Neill to resign from the Orange Order to show that he was the Prime Minister of all the people. The launching of street marches by the Northern Ireland Civil Rights Association in 1968 could be seen as a logical step after calls for reform ended, but it divided the Liberals, and McElroy himself was against mass marches as he knew it was more difficult to get people off the streets than it had been to get them on in the first place. Although O'Neill played on divisions amongst left-wing parties to win the 1965 Stormont election, he did not promote sufficiently far reaching reforms early enough to avert a turn to street politics.

Chapter Three *The Campaign for Social Justice and the Campaign for Democracy in Ulster* documents that the Campaign for Social Justice was instrumental in founding the Northern Ireland Civil Rights Association some years later, and helped prepare the ground for a mass civil rights movement. Dungannon saw a major battle over housing, and the author sees the formation of the Homeless Citizens' League as significant for the development of the civil rights movement in a number of ways. The chapter concludes that the civil rights movement felt that O'Neill was unwilling to make substantial changes and was a prisoner of the Orange Order and the Ulster Unionist Party.

Chapter Four: *The Northern Ireland Civil Rights Association* was the most important group within the civil rights movement and Purdie outlines that republicans were active in influencing the direction taken by NICRA as well as its creation. He argues that republicans were keen to push the civil rights agitation further and use it to build a radical coalition which would set its sights eventually on a united Ireland. In part, republicans saw the civil rights movement as at least a means of achieving the legalisation of republican political activity. Purdie highlights that although republicans were influential in steering the association towards public marches, the form which NICRA took was determined by the coalition of forces which actually came together to create it, and republicans were only one element of this.

Purdie contends that by 1968, NICRA believed that only public marches could draw attention to the situation. The author describes the NICRA march from Coalisland in the summer of 1968, which involved 2,000 people accompanied by nationalist bands. Purdie believes that NICRA was unwilling to accept that its marches should be treated as sectarian and provocative. Purdie argues that before the events in Derry Londonderry on 5 October the civil rights movement did not exist, they were rather a small group of activists. After this event the political situation was transformed, and media images of police batoning demonstrators increased nationalist discontent, while at the same time gave Ian Paisley the opportunity to put himself at the head of the resistance to the civil rights movement.

Chapter Five *Derry and its Action Committee* suggests that the 5 October march was not the first attempt to organise around the issue in Derry Londonderry. The Derry Unemployed Action Committee set up in 1965 was the forerunner to the Derry Housing Action Committee, which became the most important of these groupings as it was the catalyst which turned the civil rights movement into a mass campaign. The Derry Citizens' Action Committee took over from these groups and succeeded in attracting radicals and more militant elements. DCAC organised a mass sit-down in Guildhall Square, and Purdie highlights that good organisation, popular support and collaboration with the police enabled DCAC to protest peacefully and responsibility, emphasising the positive the role that can be played by good stewarding. However, by 1969 DCAC's unity had crumbled and March 1969 was the last time that DCAC could peacefully organise a mass demonstration.

Chapter Six *The People's Democracy* notes that the events of 5 October 1968 created a mass movement, but they also initiated the processes which were to lead to its dissolution. Purdie sees the People's Democracy as distinctive to the NICRA, and argues that they were almost as hostile to NICRA and DCAC as they were to the unionist government. In early 1969 the PD organised a Belfast to Derry Londonderry march when forty PD supporters set off from the city hall. At Dungiven they were confronted by a hostile crowd of about one hundred and fifty people and the marchers were attacked with stones, bottles and other projectiles. It became apparent that a local Orange Hall had been used to store and distribute cudgels, and many of the attackers were local people who were also members of the B-Specials. Terence O'Neill condemned the march to Derry Londonderry as irresponsible, while Brian Faulkner considered the march to be deliberatively provocative.

The chapter notes Bernadette Devlin's view that one factor in marching was to relaunch the civil rights movement as a mass movement. Although the marchers knew there would in all likelihood be trouble, they wanted to expose what they perceived to be the problems inherent in Northern Irish society. Similarly, Michael Farrell saw the Belfast to Derry Londonderry march as modelled on Martin Luther King's Selma to Montgomery march of 1966, and felt that the march would force the government to confront loyalists, or at least drop their pretensions about reform. When legal and political channels were closed, Purdie asserts that the civil rights movement took to the streets as a substitute for the constitutional battle.

The book concludes that in retrospect the decision of the civil rights movement to turn to street demonstrations in the summer of 1968 was a fateful one. Purdie contends that the black civil rights model of the USA was inappropriate, and street marches in Northern Ireland had a very different historical and sectarian significance, which had the potential to upset the tacit understanding between the two communities about territorial divisions. He asks why the civil rights movement did not foresee the effects of its tactics, and argues that the tactics of marches arose out of a particular situation in Dungannon when a local campaign for better housing linked up with a small civil liberties group looking for some way to make an impact. Once the civil rights leadership went onto the streets at the head of a mass movement, it drew on support which was not necessarily committed to its worldview. The civil rights leaders were not blind to the dangers of the tactics, but by the time they were apparent it was too late to turn back, and the civil rights movement ultimately failed as a collective entity, as did its individual components.

79. **Quigley, Sir George (2002)** *Report: Review of the Parades Commission and Public Processions (Northern Ireland) Act 1998.* **Belfast, No Publisher.**

This report reviews the operation of the Parades Commission and the legislation under which it was established, and considers if any changes could increase public confidence on all sides and the resolution of the parades issue peacefully. The report contends that there needs to be support for mediation to achieve a local settlement rather than a formal determination, and that there is a need for determinations to be made more transparent. The report suggests that there are difficulties with the role of the Parades Commission's Authorised Officers and their role in shuttle diplomacy, and is critical of the 'detached' status of the AOs which can give rise to an ambivalent situation whereby the actions of the AOs may not commend themselves to someone already predisposed against the Parades Commission.

It is argued that good faith efforts directed towards finding local accommodation are the most effective way of defusing community tensions and of improving relationships within the community, with the report stating that a body looking at parades should have a stronger facilitation function than it has at present. It is argued that the current situation, which relies on a third party to make determinations, hinders relationship development by producing a 'win' or 'lose' result between the two sides. Quigley contends that the current body's facilitation and determination functions should remain separate. He recommends the establishment of a separate Parades Facilitation Agency, which would be responsible for the Guidelines, Procedural Rules, Codes of Conduct, Monitoring and Education. The Commission should also revise its Code of Conduct and bring in legislation to deal with alcohol as is the case in the rest of the UK.

The Parades Commission's decision-making criteria are seen as too complex and insufficiently clear, which leads to difficulties for organisations in seeking to discover the reasons for the determinations. Quigley argues that Section 8 (6) of the 1998 Public Processions (Northern Ireland) Act should be modelled on Article 11 of the European Convention on Human Rights. The report also claims that the 1998 Human Rights Act elevated 'traditionality' to a level of importance not accorded by North in his report. The report proposes to drop the current exceptions to customarily held parades as this runs counter to equality considerations.

The report has reservations about the current decision-making process, its lack of transparency and lack of confidentiality and Quigley contends that there should be a public hearing at which parties can explore each other's positions. Greater transparency in the process and in the explanations of decisions would lead to fewer of the charges of inconsistency which at present come from both sides of the debate.

The report proposes that a Rights Panel should be the body that makes determinations, with all other matters relating to parades falling within the remit of a Parades Facilitation Agency. The Rights Panel should have no role in monitoring as this could damage the trust between the facilitation function and its clients. This facilitation function would build trust and confidence through a mediation process, and agreements reached at this facilitation stage should be written down and formally registered to avoid any misunderstandings.

The report recommends that the Public Processions (Northern Ireland) Act 1998 should be amended in line with Article 11 (1) of the ECHR. The determining body should be empowered to make rulings for periods of up to five years, while the organisers of parades should notify their intention to parade no later than 1 October every year, and no less than six months before a parade is due to take place. Protest meetings should also be under the scope of the determining body, and the Code of Conduct should require that the organiser of a parade should be clearly identified. The organiser should prepare a risk assessment for each parade, and all marshals are to receive training while parade organisers are to discuss with police where marshals' and police responsibilities are to be demarcated.

A separate Rights Panel should be established and should be the determining body with regard to parades and protests. Quigley suggests that it is possible to assess the extent to which a parade would affect the rights and freedoms of others by considering five broad areas including the nature of the parade, arrangements for the parade, characteristics of the contested part of the route, potential for disruption and any other matter concerning international human rights agreements.   The publication concludes that the facilitation and determination functions of the proposed new bodies must be kept independent of one another; otherwise the facilitation process could be compromised and the determination function would have a difficulty in refuting the charge that it was not being objective and was simply an extension of the 'settlement' process.

80. **Radford, Katy (2001) Drum Rolls and Gender Roles in Protestant Marching Bands in Belfast.** *British Journal of Ethnomusicology,* **Volume 10, Number 2.**

In this article, Radford examines how loyalist marching bands are also markers of political culture and barometers of locally controlled political power from an inter-community perspective. The article also addresses issues of gender discrimination in band membership, organization and patronage, and suggests that the bands are one way in which women can be publicly subordinated within working class Protestant culture. The paper looks at how different bands, one an accordion band, the other a 'Blood and Thunder' band, express different aspects of loyalism and transmit their value system not only to neighbouring Catholics, but also to those within the Protestant community.

Radford begins by providing a brief overview of the struggle over territorial rights in Northern Ireland, and argues that the soundscape is less fixed than the visual images of murals and flags which demarcate territory. The music of the bands crosses the boundaries into the territory of the 'other', and the music played is often threatening. She draws on previous work by de Rosa and notes the difference between the 'majorette' style of the bands of the Ancient Order of Hibernians and the militaristic re-enactment of loyalist and republican paramilitary bands. The chapter discusses the role of the 'Blood and Thunder' bands, which are often paramilitary funded and linked, and their members, who regularly jeer and taunt the 'other'. Radford describes this as analogous to the tradition of charivari or 'rough music', which has historically been widespread in Europe, and which has relied on a taunting or marginalizing of outsiders. There is also an attempt within communities to drown out the other band, perhaps associated with a rival paramilitary organisation.

Radford examines various reasons for the decline in the presence of mixed gender bands in Belfast, and focuses on the Prince William Accordion Band and the Pride of the Shankill flute band as two different examples of musical tradition within the band genre. Radford argues that the increase in 'Blood and Thunder' bands is one of the manifestations of loyalist dissatisfaction, and asserts that often the media misrepresent the situation and portray all bands as the same, which is not the case. Within the 'Blood and Thunder' bands women are seen in a subordinate role and even the instruments they use are subject to male approval and are based on gendered notions. Radford contests a militant affirmation of Protestant identity as the bands' sole raison d'etre, and suggests that through rehearsals and performance these bands are also used to instil a sense of musical tradition.

81. **Radford, Katy (2004) Protestant Women - Protesting Faith: Tangling Secular and Religious Identity in Northern Ireland. In Coleman, Simon and Collins, Peter (eds.)** *Religion, Identity and Change.* **Aldershot, Ashgate.**

This chapter describes events at Drumcree from the experiences of a group of Protestant women from the Shankill Road in Belfast and explores their experiences of the protest at Drumcree from a gendered perspective. Radford also attempts to highlight the interdependence between secular and devout religious practices within political and religious rituals in Northern Ireland. A brief consideration of the role of the church parade from the perspective of the Loyal Orders is provided to partly explain the significance of their stance at Drumcree. Radford implies that the line between raucous secular parades and mild mannered church parades has been blurred by the Drumcree dispute.

She discusses the Shankill Women Support Drumcree Group, and describes the women's presence at Drumcree as tolerated, and a presence that stresses the women's domesticity. The chapter argues that once co-opted, women have invariably subordinated issues of particular interest to them to the pursuance of sectarian ideology. The media coverage of Drumcree focuses on conservative expectations of women within the community, and reinforces the women's lack of agency and the view that their roles are passive. Radford asserts that the role of women in the Drumcree dispute fails to challenge the patriarchal status quo, and that the parts played by women in Orange ritual are simultaneously integral and peripheral. She concludes that the Orangemen and their supporters at Drumcree are undermining their own position, and the role of secular and not religious loyalism weakens Orangemen's claims of pursuing 'religious and civil liberty'.

82. Ryder, Chris and Kearney, Vincent (2001) *Drumcree: The Orange Order's Last Stand*. London, Methuen.

Ryder and Kearney discuss various Drumcree disputes and argue that the seeds for Drumcree were sown in 1985 with Protestant opposition to the nationalist St. Patrick's Day parade in Portadown. While noting that marching has been a predominant feature of life and political expression in Northern Ireland, the authors suggest that it has also been the source of trouble, violence and regular deaths. The handful of contentious parades where trouble occurs has the potential to bring Northern Ireland to a stand-still and to create full-scale political crises, and this the authors argue is exactly what happened at Drumcree in 1996.

The book provides some background to the formation of the Orange Order and documents historic disturbances that have occurred at parades throughout the years. The authors claim that various laws attempting to regulate parades over the years have had little impact on the 'Orange Citadel', and that while nationalists have focused on the unacceptability of annual marches in the Tunnel area and Obins Street, the Orange Order has defended their 'traditional' routes, with any concession seen to affect marches elsewhere in Northern Ireland.

The 1980s saw an increasing willingness on the part of the RUC to face up to the Orange Order in terms of their parade routes, and the blocking of a nationalist parade in 1985 in Portadown led many nationalist residents to feel that there should never be another Orange parade in their area again. Against the backdrop of increasing violence, 1987 was the first year since the war years that the Orange Order chose not to go to Drumcree church. Ryder and Kearney examine the increasing nationalist protests against parades in the 1990s after the 1994 paramilitary ceasefires. These moves caused concern amongst Orange leaders, and the authors outline Jeffrey Donaldson's view that if the Orange Order lost out in Portadown, they would lose out everywhere else, and they were determined to defend their civil and religious liberty.

The events of Drumcree from 1995 onwards are discussed in some detail and the book contends that nationalist opposition to parades was not simply a republican plot. The second dispute at Drumcree in 1996 is said to have led to a complete meltdown of community relationships and shattered nationalist confidence in the RUC. Ryder and Kearney highlight that the replacement of the RUC directly flows from events at Drumcree in 1996.

The book concludes that Drumcree had a far more debilitating impact on the Orange Order than they had realised, and that many liberals and traditionalists even left the Institution over the dispute. The economic and social costs of Drumcree are discussed, with Ryder and Kearney outlining that events at Drumcree had cost the Northern Ireland economy at least £40 million in lost tourism revenue, £50 million in policing costs, and £166 million in criminal damage costs since 1995. They conclude that the problem of Drumcree is perhaps so intractable due to the distinctive nature of Portadown itself as the 'Orange Citadel'.

83. Salhany, Susan (2007) *Exposing Foucault's Two Rituals: Considering the Symbolic Dimension of Government.* **Ottawa, Carelton University.**

This article suggests that rituals and symbols may be the object of government and may be taken up in strategies to identify and calculate the conduct of individuals and groups. Salhany principally addresses Foucault's 'Discipline and Punish' work in relation to the Parades Commission in Northern Ireland, and argues that rituals remained tied to the sovereign exercise of power. When considering the work of the Parades Commission from a government perspective it becomes apparent that ritual and symbolic practices may be taken up outside sovereignty and within the 'art of governing'. Salhany sees the Parades Commission's attempts to remove sectarian symbols, language and music from parades as an attempt to transform and shape the symbolic meaning of the parade and avoid the provocation of violence. The Commission does this in an attempt to create shared meaning among Catholics and Protestants about the parades. She concludes that parades are a site of struggle between the loyalist groups, nationalist groups and formal state authorities such as the Parades Commission, and that the ritual parades continue to mark those involved as individuals in their constitution as religious, ethnic and gendered political subjects.

84. Tonkin, Elizabeth and Bryan, Dominic (1996) Political Ritual: Temporality and Tradition. In Boholm, Asa (ed.) *Political Ritual*. Gothenburg, Institute for Advanced Studies in Social Anthropology.

This edited volume contains contributions from the Institute for Advanced Studies in Social Anthropology's Summer Conference of June 1994. The book explores the ways in which people deal with symbols and how they then use them in contexts of power within the semantics of their cultural system.

Chapter One *Political Ritual: Temporality and Tradition* focuses on ritual as performance proclaiming some state of authority as a 'timeless' act. The chapter uses Orange commemorations in Northern Ireland and West African rituals as case studies, outlining that there is much more to Twelfth of July rituals than is usually acknowledged. Tonkin and Bryan describe the Twelfth parade and highlight the development of the more raucous 'Kick the Pope' bands over the last twenty years. The event itself gives the appearance of stasis, and Tonkin and Bryan argue that it is easy to conclude that there is no dynamic change in the codes used for communication.

The chapter discusses the impact the collapse of Stormont rule in 1972 had on increasing Protestant alienation from the British state, and notes a difference between the senior Orangemen who attempt to derive legitimacy through parades and speeches and the people who march behind them. The authors chart the breakdown in 'hegemonic' unionism from the middle of the Twentieth Century which subsequently has led to a breakdown in consensus over the meaning of the Twelfth itself, with historical discontent amongst working class unionism towards the 'elite' who attempt to use the power of the ritual for other political ends.

The importance of repetition is said to be vital, as the recurring symbols provide a sense of unity and stability and assert the continuing power of unionism. Tonkin and Bryan highlight that despite this, the Orange Order themselves continually struggle to control the parades and their meaning. It is contended that in times of uncertainty and conflict, one should expect ritual authority to be both exploited and contested by a number of different participants. The chapter highlights the paradox within ritual performances in events such as the Twelfth, as it is both temporal and traditional. The authors conclude that the rituals ultimately have to change in order to survive and respond to events in a given political context.

85. United States Institute of Peace (no date) *Simulation on Northern Ireland: One Step at a Time – The Derry March and Prospects for Peace.* **www.usip.org. (Accessed May 2007)**

This article documents a simulation on marches in Derry Londonderry, and focuses on the arguments for and against whether the Parades Commission should allow a Loyal Order parade in Derry Londonderry. Participants are invited to play the roles of representatives of the various political parties, associations and government authorities, and the exercise aims to promote improved understanding of the conflict and the possibility of finding new proposals to resolve parading disputes.

86. Walker, Brian (1996) *Dancing to History's Tune: History, Myth and Politics in Ireland.* **Belfast, Institute of Irish Studies.**

Chapter Five: *Commemorations, festivals and public holidays* looks at ritual events and how their meanings have altered over time. Walker begins by focusing on the changes that have taken place in the St. Patrick's Day parade over the years, with renewed interest in the 1970s and 1980s in Catholic areas of the North. The chapter notes that even Belfast Orangemen took part in a St. Patrick's Day parade along the Shankill Road in 1985, while in 1994 the St. Patrick's flag flew over the Orange Order's Headquarters for the first time. The section also traces the development of commemorations of the Easter Rising, and suggests that the outbreak of the Troubles in 1969 cast a shadow over the celebrations, which were traditionally confined to nationalist areas and primarily West Belfast. Walker also examines the development of the Twelfth of July over the years, claiming that in the last three decades of the nineteenth century the size of the parades increased, and that they became more respectable and more linked to political unionism. Since 1969, disputes over marching routes have become a cause of riot and conflict in some areas, especially where there has been a change in population, and the chapter questions whether or not the Twelfth in recent years is more of a political or a cultural event.

87. Witherow, Jacqueline (2005) *The 'War on Terrorism' and Protestant Parading Bands in Northern Ireland.* **Available online at http://www.qub.ac.uk/sites/QUEST/FileStore/Filetoupload ,25795,en.pdf**

This brief paper presents the view that after the attacks of 9/11, paramilitary groups in Northern Ireland were forced to rethink their strategies and seek alternative methods of demonstrating their continued existence and potential manpower. This is said to be the case particularly in the Protestant community and is highlighted by the rise in band traditions. As paramilitary activity has become less acceptable, there has been a rapid rise in parading band traditions. Witherow provides a short overview of parading and highlights that prior to World War Two band membership was within the Orange Order itself, but after the war bands slowly became independent of the lodges. The paper draws on Dominic Bryan's work and argues that the growth in band competitions from the 1960s has established clear identities for the bands, making them distinct from the Orange Order. The rise of 'Blood and Thunder' flute bands is seen in part as a general disaffection with the Orange Order's perceived inability to provide security during the Troubles, and the bands are said to have varying degrees of links with various loyalist paramilitary organisations. The paper argues that many bands are an outlet for an expression of political discontent for young males, and the author believes that the bands are strongest in enclave and border areas where people feel most vulnerable.

The peace process is discussed briefly, and the author states that the loyalist paramilitary ceasefire led to a need for young loyalists to reassert their position, and that subsequently this period saw the growth of flute bands in working class loyalist areas. The development of the bands is charted, and the paper asserts that as they have attempted to become more 'respectable', there have been offers from non-governmental organisations and the government as an incentive for further 'band development'. This it is hoped will reduce some bands' dependence on paramilitaries for financial support. The document concludes that the 'War on Terror' led to paramilitarism becoming less acceptable, and that the flute bands stepped into the breach and became the defenders of communities. Witherow argues that the marching bands have become 'Peace Process Soldiers', both audibly and visibly defending Protestant parades while at the same time demonstrating their strength in terms of manpower.